Stuck on the Couch

by

James H. Kirklin II

2475 Cobb Pkwy Unit #412

Smyrna, GA 30080

678-732-5440

revjhk7@gmail.com

Contents

Printed in the United States of America

First Printing, 2024

ISBN: 979-8-218-42748-1

Published by PL Publishing

Dedication

First, I give honor to God, Who is the head of my life; to Jesus the Christ, sole mediator between God and man; and, with special recognition, to the Holy Ghost, Who is my guide.

I dedicate this book in loving memory to my late mom, Karen LaRue Kirklin. I wish she were here to witness this accomplishment; she was there every step of the way. To my parents, James and Phyllis Kirklin, and to my children – James III (Tré), Kennedy, and McKenzie - who have helped to make me the man that I am, this is for you.

To all the spiritual ravens God sent while I was stuck on the couch: Pastor Greg, Keith, Lakeesha, Katrina, Pastor Evins, and a host of unnamed angels...Thank you!!!

And to the men and women who might be "stuck " right now on a couch of their own, I pray that my journey will inspire your journey, and then usher you forward on *your* path to better.

/jhk

Foreword

After more than 30 years working in the mental health profession, it is not uncommon for me to encounter people who are simply "stuck." The work of the mental health professional is to assist people with getting "un-stuck." Rev. James H. Kirklin II, friend and fellow minister, experienced a series of life events that resulted in his being "stuck on the couch." But through bold self-reflection, self-evaluation and self-development, James was able to release himself from that position! Now, with remarkable transparency, he shares that journey and the steps he took to regain his life and walk into a brighter future. James bravely puts in writing what most people never divulge, a thought-provoking, inspiring, and hope-filled adventure!

Come along with Rev. James as he recounts the journey that forever changed his life!

Rev. Rayfield Evins, Jr.

For the last 15 years, Rev. Ray Evins, Jr., has served as pastor of Southside Missionary Baptist Church in Columbus, MS. In addition, Rev. Evins has worked 30 years in the mental health field, and currently is Executive Director of Community Counseling Services, West Point, MS.

Editor's Eye...

Rev. James,

Reviewing this copy with you will be fun, and because you and I go back "a mighty long way," Memory Lane is a good place to start. I will continue to play my role, of course, but you bring that deep valley experience and faith-earned wisdom to which this current generation and (we) older folks can relate.

Overall, what I see is a manuscript that opens in the present, travels back in time for context, then returns to the present by way of a remarkable journey. Along the way, you learn some stuff the hard way, sharing your evolution with readers through trips down Memory Lane, intimate narratives, church chronicles, raucous laughter, heartbreaking tears, Bible study, and historical snapshots.

You present yourself a transparent maze of contradictions: saint and sinner, honest and deceitful, strong and fragile, intelligent and foolish, rich and poor, loved and loving, grown and growing...in other words, human.

Truly you have been faithful over a few things. Your readers will be enlightened and inspired by life lessons from a man committed to an ordained destination where life is worth emulating.

Congratulations!

Rev. Monifa A. Jumanne, Ph.D.

Editor

Now, I'm Ready

Can I be honest? Writing this book has been a struggle with a capital S. My plan was to be finished a year ago, but I fell short of that goal. Maybe I sabotaged myself, because I would develop writing plans, get in a good rhythm, write 30 or 40 pages, and then come to a screeching halt. I thought I was clearly and effectively conveying the message. Invariably, though, I would find myself in a rut with unpredictably long dry spells. Eventually, I would learn that I was living incomplete chapters.

That is exactly what I was doing, living this thing called life - all of it. Life was happening whether I wanted to take part or not. I say this because on many days I checked out, but life kept happening. Why? Because even though I lost sight of my purpose, my purpose had not lost sight of me. Therefore, I had to go through a process to get back on the path to better. Life kept happening and God kept sending reminders of who I am and who He called me to be.

Sometimes going through the "process" felt like surgery without anesthesia. I felt every incision, every suture. I heard the doctors diagnosing my situation. I was aware, but not coherent. I was marinating in misery, not realizing that God was imparting valley tactics. That's the part I didn't highlight enough- the fact that God kept me while I was in that valley.

Writing portions of this book caused me to visit parts of my past that I didn't realize were traumatic. Like the time I withdrew the right hand of fellowship from my lifelong best friend D; I just moved on. Everyone needs a friend in whom they can confide. In every instance, I just moved on, which is not the healthiest foundation from which to write. Therefore, I'm writing this first portion of the book at the end, because most of the book was complete when I wrote this portion. That's a good thing. Please don't think I'm crazy. I'm not. Instead, I'm finally whole enough to tell my story my way. Told too soon, it might have done more harm than good. I heard a writing coach tell her students to be careful when writing their stories, because sometimes we unintentionally bleed on our audiences. I was bleeding profusely, internally. My audience would have gotten a very tainted story because I was not yet healed. My sores were very much internal. The goal of a sore is to become a scar. First, it's a painful sore, then a scab, which becomes a painless scar. That's when the sore is finally healed. I am proud to say that today, at the age of 51, I am healed, whole, and living my best life.

For the better part of five years, I pressed life's pause button and stayed stuck – on the couch. When I first started writing, I had gotten off the couch physically, but not mentally. I was still a victim of "stinking thinking." Although I enhanced my home aesthetically when I replaced my old couch with a new one, not much else had changed. Changing the furniture often requires adding accessories. Perhaps, before bringing in furniture, the carpet needs to be cleaned or the floor needs to be waxed. I recently upgraded my home using this formula: first prepare the room. Before I moved new furniture into my new place, I had the walls painted. When I moved a new living room set into my old place, I'm not sure I prepared for it. That was like putting new wine in old wineskins.

That's the thing; you can't put new wine in an old wineskin without encountering problems. If you're going to present new wine, put it in a new wineskin. Old wineskins tend to harden, which creates cracks and crevices invisible to the naked eye. When the new wine is poured in, it may leak through those cracks. New wineskin is more pliable than the old, so there is less likelihood of cracks and crevices. Therefore, the new wine will be safe and preserved.

I put new furniture in my home, but still had an old mindset. Externally things looked better, but internally, I was the same person with the same unhealthy, unhealed thoughts. I hadn't done the necessary work to move towards proper healing, and this was evident in my writing. Thankfully, the steps of a good man are ordered by the Lord (Psalm 37:23). I must have still qualified because I ended up right where I needed to be. My path might not have been traditional, but it was my path. We all have our own personal path, and as peculiar as mine might have been, it was mine. One pastor told me I was taking the wilderness route to healing and wholeness.

I did not take the normal steps that many potential divorcees take. I didn't go to counseling. I didn't join support groups. I didn't ingratiate myself into social activities. I was single, now. Imagine that. I could do whatever I wanted. If I wanted to go out and meet a bunch of women, I could. If I wanted to be alone, I had that choice, as well. Loneliness made me want company, but I needed more than just company. I needed completion and that wasn't going to come in the form of a companion. So, finding a new woman was not a priority. The number one priority was finding myself. That was the priority. I had to become reacquainted with James Kirklin II to remind him that his purpose is bigger than his problems. I had to find me. If I found me again, I would also find the foundation for becoming a better version of myself.

That was not easy. I had become a very different person over the last 25 years. But in the last 5 years, I lost a part of myself. I made a slew of bad decisions, some out of fear, others because I was among the walking wounded. In public, I looked like everything was all right, but inside, I was hemorrhaging, silently suffering, but too proud to admit it. Friends came and left. I ran some of them away. I'm sorry if you're on that list. I was not in a healthy place and wanted to be left alone. I did not want to be bothered by anyone. I continued to trust God because that was my only option. Everyone and everything left me (I have come to discover that this was part of His plan). The Lord never left me; he kept my mind intact. Still, I experienced some very lonesome moments. I mean, I was painfully lonely. Silence and noise were synonymous. And in those moments, I listened intently to make sure I heard the Shepherd's voice (John 10:27), because several voices were speaking. At times, he spoke in a whisper; at other times, loud and commanding, but I recognized His voice. Most important to me is that, throughout the chaos and the changes, He kept speaking.

God inspired me to start the Intellectual Stew, a weekly podcast I do live on Facebook and YouTube. Little did I know when I started that that platform would be a very public form of therapy. I used the issues I was going through as topics for my weekly show. Then, I would invite people who had experienced similar circumstances to tell their stories. If I did it right, listeners would pick up nuggets of wisdom to nurture them through their dilemmas. The countless number of emails and phone calls I receive telling me how the conversations helped them, let me know the tactic is effective.

Some people might say I was being too honest. But part of the reason I started the podcast was that I knew my ex-wife was listening. I figured if she heard me publicly acknowledge my faults, that she would see my humility and more importantly, hear my heart. She would literally hear me pour my heart out in front of the world, acknowledging my mistakes and esteeming her every chance I got. I fell on a very public sword, taking responsibility for where I was in life. I spoke as though the divorce was 100% my fault. Now I have come to discover that that was not necessarily the case. We both played a part.

I longed for companionship but had not given myself permission to move on. Women listening to my podcast would not take me seriously because they thought I was still in love with my ex, based on how I spoke on the podcast. You could not get me to say a negative thing about her. All my examples included some reference to that relationship. We shared 20 years of history, and all that history wasn't bad. Most people speak from the context of their experience, and that was the only marital experience I had. So, that was all I knew to speak about.

The truth is those women were right. Don't tell them I said this. If they confront me, I will deny it. But seriously, some of them were spot on. I was still in love and that love limited me from moving forward and exploring available options. I came to discover that it wasn't important for me to move on to someone else. I needed to move forward for myself. Talk about being stuck on Barely Get Along Blvd. and Enough Avenue. That was my new neighborhood. Thankfully, it was temporary. You see, it's one thing to be in a bad place, physically, but it's worse when you're there mentally. And that's exactly where I was-stuck in a state of stagnation. I desperately needed to form new habits.

The idea that it takes 21 days to form a habit comes from the book, "*Psycho-Cybernetics,*" by plastic surgeon Dr. Maxwell Maltz in the 1950s. However, this number was not based on scientific research and is now considered a myth. The time it takes to form a habit can vary significantly depending on the individual, the behavior being adopted, and the circumstances. Recent research suggests that it may take much longer to form a habit, with studies showing an average of 66 days or more. According to a study published in the *European Journal of Social Psychology* in 2009, the time needed to form a habit ranged from 18 to 254 days, with the median being 66 days. However, some participants in the study took much longer, so there is no fixed number of days that applies to everyone. The key to forming a habit is consistency and repetition.

The more consistently and persistently one engages in a behavior, the more likely it is to become a habit. This varies based on the complexity of the habit and individual differences. For instance, simple habits may develop more quickly than complex ones. I am not sure on which chronological day I formed my bad habit; I just know that I did. I believe I formed my habit on the first day and just ended up doing the same thing, repeating the same negative behavior for multiple years. At that point, it escalated from being a habit to being a lifestyle.

As you read farther, you will learn how I moved out of my house and into my apartment on Sunday. Then, I went to work on Monday and was told that my services were no longer needed. I was recently divorced and had become accustomed to two incomes. Now, I had my own responsibilities with no job. Immediately, I made a vow. I told myself that I would never again give anyone the power to fire me. When I make a vow to myself, I keep it. I also said that I would never again work for a dealership. I understand that Georgia is a right to fire State, but this dealership said I was let go because I didn't smile enough. Well, who smiles while they are involuntarily going through a divorce? So, they fired me. Looking back on it, I am not sure if that was the real reason I was let go. Honestly, I just don't think I fit in that environment. That was proven when I tried to go back to work.

Because I thought I was healed from that situation, I broke my own rule and went back to work at a dealership. Sales were going okay, but could have been much better. I had only sold a handful of cars in the 20+ days I was there. That certainly wasn't the plan. I thought I would go in and immediately sell 15-20 cars a month and make 10-15k a month. Keep in mind that during this time, every automobile manufacturer was experiencing inventory shortages. Not to mention that we were selling cars for thousands of dollars over the sticker price, and the sales culture wasn't the most inviting, I was not as successful as I would have liked. So, I was already questioning my decision. As time would have it, one day the manager gave one of those fiery speeches where he motivated people by demotivating them and threatening to fire everyone for every little thing if they didn't sell more cars. And then he said those magic words, if you take your day off and only have X number of cars sold, you are fired. I think my spirit heard what my ears did not: a subliminal threat. I have never been one to respond positively to tough love. I didn't realize it at the time, but somewhere in the middle of his soliloquy, I checked out. Subconsciously, I started to plan my exit. That was on a Monday. God sent a life raft in the form of a contract gig that would start that Thursday. I quit Wednesday and went back to doing contract gigs. In the book, you will understand how God sustained me all those years, even when I appeared to be stuck.

As I take you on a journey through my experiences on the couch, I need you to view them through lenses that are healed. Cloudy or foggy lenses might have given you a limited view. You may identify with the story but not rejoice in the glory that came out of it. Foggy lenses will have you focusing on the losses, causing you to miss out on the lessons. Life certainly lent its share of lessons. When I emerged from my pity party, I was able to consider the clues and get on the path to better. In fact, this became my mantra. I created a hashtag, #OnThePathToBetter. I printed it on T-shirts and sweatpants. It scrolls across the bottom of the screen on my podcast. I have done shows about it. I even ask a very specific question in the introduction to the video of my show, How are you going to do better if you don't know what better looks like? I knew what it looked like but wasn't showing it. So, how was I going to tell people to do better if I wasn't willing to do the work to present a better version of myself?

Authenticity attracts and people recognize when a person is not operating in their own truism. I was presenting what I had left in the tank, but it was not my best. I had to change that by changing my behavior. I even changed how I dressed. My daily wardrobe consisted of clothes displaying my hashtag. If I went to the grocery store, I had on a T-shirt. If I was just lounging around the house, I wore one of my T-shirts. If I went to lunch or breakfast with my pastor, I wore one of my T-shirts. Unbeknownst to me, my merch was more than just merch. I was a walking billboard for others, as well as myself. This ministry had been ministering to me, reminding me that better existed and that there was a path to get there. I just had to be willing to get on it. Not only that, but I had to be willing to stay on it until I reached my destination. Every time I looked in the mirror, I was reminded. Whenever someone struck up a conversation about it, those were reminders. Thank God for reminders. Reminders help us remember and as I remembered, I started thinking, Hello, James... WELCOME BACK!

Let's talk about what reminders do for us. In short, reminders make life easier. The human mind is fallible and susceptible to error, making it easy to forget appointments, deadlines, tasks, and events. Reminders help bridge this gap by providing external cues that trigger the memory. The enemy does not want us to remember because we will see who we are supposed to be and walk towards our purpose. That is why we are encouraged to stay focused. Once lost, focus is hard to get back. Believe me. I know. It's a good thing to have reminders. As I incorporate them into my routine, they help with time management, event notification, completing projects, keeping up with doctor's appointments, and reducing stress, among other things. Google and I converse often, and she keeps me in the know regarding my schedule. The constant reminders that I was on the path to better assured me that a better way was within reach. I just had to be willing to take steps in the right direction, and the first step...was to forgive myself.

Listen... I will discuss all these things. I just felt like I needed to supply a bit of healthy context before we move ahead on the journey, which starts on one couch and ends on another. The second couch was bought brand new and is in its place, ready to create its own culture. Let's see how we got here...

Introduction: How Did I Get Here?

A popular old saying is, "Hindsight is 20/20 vision." If we had the ability to know what will happen in the future, we would find ourselves in possession of a game changer. It would be synonymous with living with a loaded deck and we would have an invaluable advantage. Unfortunately, such is not the case. In the real world, we live our lives day by day, moment by moment, until our time on Earth expires. When we do it right, we reap rewards. When we do it wrong, we're often forced to face uncomfortable circumstances. When we make bad decisions, we must be accountable for our actions.

A few years ago, I found myself in this unwanted, but well-deserved, position. I felt that everything I was going through was my fault. I experienced a myriad of emotions: shame, guilt, feelings of inadequacy, and lack of self-worth, among them. That was a dark time for me; I would not wish those feelings on my worst enemy. So, it is my desire that all who read these words will learn from my mistakes. Perhaps, some young man is considering an action that would jeopardize his marriage by thinking with the wrong head. It is my desire that after reading these words, he will make a wiser decision.

Then, there's the gentleman, who, like me – was stuck on the couch, marinating in his own misery, feeling sorry for himself. Perhaps, after reading these words, that individual will find within himself the strength to get off the couch and do a personal assessment. After detecting his flaws, that individual would make the necessary adjustments. He will do whatever is necessary, except stay stuck on the couch.

And then there is the woman who reads this story and becomes enlightened and perhaps, will better understand her man. She might realize that men can grow up in a marriage. The key is to grow together. I obviously failed because I am here, stuck on the couch, sharing my experiences.

This is my story...

You could not have told me that I wasn't having a nightmare. At any moment, the alarm clock would go off and I would wake up. Sadly, I was not dreaming; I was very much awake. It was not a dream, and my salvation was not coming in the form of an alarm clock. This dream, no, this nightmare, was my present reality. This was my new lot in life, the cards have been dealt, and this was the hand I had been left to play. For the first time in over 20 years, I was alone. I was literally by myself. Who would have "thunk" it? If someone had told me five years ago that I'd be alone like this, I would have vehemently disagreed. If someone had told me the day before, or even the very day I heard the words that pierced my heart and changed, no, shattered life as I knew it, I would have called them a bald-faced liar. However, my present circumstances reveal that the hands of time have transitioned, bringing undesired, yet inevitable, change. I was alone. No wife, no children (in the home), and no dog (in the home), just me, the man in the mirror, and my thoughts- ALONE.

"Hold on."

"Wait a minute."

"How did I get here?"

These questions bombarded the forefront of my thoughts on that Sunday evening in October. The challenge was to turn this apartment into a home. The U-Haul was unloaded, piece by piece, box by box. Well, it was only one load. I only needed one because the items I did not need, either I gave away or sent to the junk yard. So, I didn't have much.

I hung my clothes in the closet, which was much smaller than the closets to which I had grown accustomed. The ones I shared with my ex-wife, Nikki, over the past 17 years were usually walk-in, and I would have my own little section in the back corner. Nikki usually dominated the space because she had more clothes. This new one was walk-in too, but it seemed empty because something was missing. It was half and not whole. It just wasn't the same.

I unloaded the furniture and placed it in the rooms that would serve as their new home. I was tasked with serving as furniture mover and interior decorator. It was just a one-bedroom apartment so there were only three or four rooms. This little one bedroom was a blessing. I was not prepared to move, so I didn't have much money.

Thankfully, I still had decent credit, so I was able to move in on a special the complex was having: no deposit and half-price rent. Old folks' say the Lord may not come when you want him to, but he's always on time. I'm a witness. And here I was trying to turn a small apartment into a home.

Starting with the bedroom, I placed the armoire against the wall, and tucked the two nightstands into separate corners. I didn't have pictures or sconces to hang on the walls like I had in the house I was accustomed to living in. I didn't even know where to buy those items. Feng shui just didn't seem all that important. The queen-sized, formal bedroom, which used to serve guests in the old house, now serves as the master in its new place. Ironically, this bed survived three moves and almost three years of storage. But this time, can you believe I broke it? During the move, the bed fell in the back of the U-Haul and one of the posts broke but didn't shatter (that's a sermon for someone). Despite its being broken, I was able to patch it together with a little creativity. You would be surprised what miracles a little Gorilla Glue and packing tape can perform.

I remember making the bed for the first time in my "new" home. The first thing I noticed was the limited options. The linen closet I was used to had multiple options of sheets - different colors, different thread counts, and multiple sizes. Ironically, when I looked this time, I only saw a couple of options and they were either beige or white. I'm not sure which color I went with, but I unfolded the fitted sheet and placed it on the bed. Then, I put on the flat sheet, making sure to properly tuck each corner as I was taught. I placed the pillowcases on the pillows and draped the comforter across the bed. This was my new bedroom. Although it was filled with furniture, it felt empty. I remember standing back and looking at my accomplishments and asking myself if this was really my new home. Little did I know it would be months before I would be able to sleep through the night in that bed. We'll get back to that in a little while.

Next, I started on the dining room, which was really just an extension of the living room. Over the years, this "formal" dining room table has served hundreds of family meals, held numerous business sessions with insurance agents, and witnessed dozens of tough love conversations. It is the table where culture was created; it would need to create a culture in its new home. The table would not have fit in that small space, so I removed the sleeve, making it shorter so that my computer desk would fit. I didn't have an office chair as I had in the old house, but the dining room chair served that dual purpose just fine.

Once I hooked up the ethernet cable, I had Internet access and was good to go. Internet access was an absolute necessity, because despite this perilous present, I was still matriculating through school and couldn't afford to let my grades drop. I set the table with the placemats I brought with me. I think I just wanted to have some semblance of home, and little things like placemats served that purpose in the beginning. I spent a lot of time at that computer.

Next, I moved on to the kitchen. I would tell you everything that was in the kitchen, but there really isn't much to tell. This was a sparse inventory, indeed: two pots, a large frying pan, one baking sheet, one cereal bowl, 3 dinner plates, a few butter knives, and a couple of forks and spoons. If memory serves me correctly, there were also a few glasses, some paper plates, and sporadic pieces of Tupperware, along with some random seasonings.

I brought items to put in the refrigerator, but only faintly remember what they were - pickles, salad dressings, maybe? The only thing I remember for sure was a bottle of Sweet Baby Ray's BBQ Sauce. I loved me some Sweet Baby Ray's. A garbage can, broom, and a bottle of Fabuloso sat near the door. Anything else I needed I'd have to buy, although I usually didn't know what I didn't have until I needed it. Few things are more inconvenient than being in the middle of cooking and realizing that the recipe calls for milk, and you don't have any. My new place was close to major grocery stores, so I made quite a few runs to the store.

On to the living room. This room had to be right because surely, I would be spending the majority of my time here. So, I put on my interior decorator hat. This was the room that would contain a gargantuan entertainment center. It also housed a 48-inch Vizio TV and served as a bookshelf and trophy case. I had a few trophies and accolades to place in their respective locations, but at this point, I really didn't feel like a winner. My entire life had changed.

The remaining furniture consisted of an old couch and a matching chair. No end tables, no lamps, not even an ottoman. I thought we had an ottoman in the earlier house. I guess not. Maybe Nikki took it, or maybe I threw it away. Nevertheless, this was all I had to work with. As I stated before, Feng shui just did not seem that important. I made sure the furniture allowed me to move freely throughout the room and enabled me to access the balcony through the sliding glass door. The entertainment center lined the only wall long enough to fit it. A small glass TV stand with three shelves is what I placed the TV on. I placed the couch directly in front of the television and kitty-cornered the chair next to it. I have no clue why I went with this design, because I made the fireplace useless, since it was behind the couch. Go figure. Again, Feng shui was not the goal. I was not trying to win an interior decorating contest. I was merely trying to adjust to life in my new home. Logistically, I was set. Everything was in place, apart from buying toilet tissue and placing my toiletries in the bathroom. All systems were Go. My address was officially changed. The home I built for the last seventeen years was a thing of the past. I had to face my present reality unless I could change her mind. I still held on to a little hope that we could reconcile.

But, nope. This was really happening. My subliminal fear had manifested. I was living, sleeping, eating, and paying bills in a house apart from the family I had spent seventeen years helping to construct. They were there and I was here. I remember sitting on that couch thinking these thoughts. The answer to my first question was incomplete. It still bombarded the forefront of my thoughts as I sat there, stuck, and I do mean stuck, on the couch. I needed an answer: "How did I get here?"

Physically, I made the transition from Kennesaw to Smyrna. I moved from the four-bedroom, 2.5-bathroom home with a fenced in backyard, to a one-bedroom apartment in an enclosed community. I could have chosen a unit with washer and dryer connections, but for what? The other unit was more expensive, and I didn't own a washer and dryer, anyway. I considered this a physical representation of where I was, but it only answered half the question. My body was in one place, but my mind was in a different place. It was only after the furniture was in place, the movers were gone, and I was left alone with my thoughts, on the couch with no cable and no Internet, that I realized mentally, I was not okay. I pinched myself, hoping I would awake from this nightmare. My mind kept telling me that I was going to have to break the lease at my new place because in a few months, Nikki would call and say that all is forgiven, and I could come home. At least, that's how it happened last time. My mind said this was just another temporary setback. Eventually, she would see that I had learned to listen and forgive me. We could then place this situation in our faith file and use it as a testimony to help struggling couples in the future.

Early on in our marriage, after a setback, Nikki forgave me and told me she believed that one day we would be able to help others who were struggling in marriage. After all, we had been married for 17 years, and during that time, I had done things that warranted my being where I was. However, I thought I had weathered those storms and honestly, I thought the statute of limitations had run out. Where we were, couples were usually able to press the cruise control button. But, month after month passed and no phone call came, no reconciliation was offered. If I were a cat, I must have been on my 10th life. It was over. I was now on the verge of officially and legally becoming a single man.

I kept asking myself, How did I get here? I didn't want to face the reality behind that answer. I was in utter disbelief. I knew in whom I had faith, but my faith was fragmented and failing. I couldn't believe God let this happen. Isn't that how some of us do it? We dig ourselves a hole or place ourselves in some precarious pit and then start to play the blame game, making God out to be the culprit or cause of our calamity. I told myself, No sir! James, this is 100% your fault. I told myself this over and over again. The enemy used these thoughts to dupe me into darkness and depression.

In the Apostle Paul's second letter to the church at Corinth, he spoke of how the god of this world had blinded the minds of certain people.

In whom the god of this world hath blinded the minds of them which believe not, lest the light of the glorious gospel of Christ, who is the image of God, should shine unto them. (2 Corinthians 4:4)

I have never been physically blind, but when I close my eyes tight, all I see is darkness. I see no light. It's hard to function when all you see is darkness. It's hard to move around. You can't read anything. You fumble around until you find a light switch, a flashlight, a candle, or something that yields light.

The enemy would be happy if we never found light again. He would prefer that we remain in dark places. But note what the apostle says that the enemy blinds. He blinds the minds, not the eyes. His mission is to disrupt thoughts and alter attitudes, causing us to focus on the wrong things and stifle our ability to produce positively. In other words, we start to take part in stinking thinking. At least, I did. I had the temerity to blame God for my decisions when I know that I deserved everything I was dealing with. I could hear the sentiments of old folks echoing in my mind: "If you lie down with dogs, you get up with fleas." "If you play with fire, you might get burned." "What's done in the dark will find its way to the light." My deeds in the dark had finally come to light. It was time to make recompense for the sins of my past.

I thought I had outlived my indiscretions. In fact, after 17 long years, I thought I had grown into the man I needed to be for my wife and for the marriage. For me, growth was a good thing. Many of the desires I had in my younger years no longer appealed to me. Honestly, I was good now and had been for a while. I was learning… No, scratch that. I finally learned what it meant to be a good husband. As odd as it may sound, being faithful felt good.

Likewise, I was learning how to be a better father behind closed doors and not just in the public eye. I was proud of James III (Tre), Kennedy and McKenzie; I owed them. I joined the parents who post their children's accomplishments on social media so they can be told what great parents they are. Well, I was a little guilty of the "My children are smarter than your children" syndrome. I posted weekly photos at the tumbling lessons with the hashtag #daddyduties. I recorded Kennedy's one-on-one hitting lessons, never failing to leave out the hashtag #daddyduties. I was putting in the work. We struggled to pay the travel ball fees and for the hitting lessons, sometimes paying them before paying the household bills, but I thought those were "daddy duties," and honestly thought those actions were buying me time. I figured if we focused on the children and invested in their success, that I would have time to fix the relationship that really needed to be fixed - the one with my spouse. We were young and by the time McKenzie was slated to graduate from high school, I wouldn't even have reached my 50th birthday. She would be even younger. Therefore, we had time. Or at least, I thought we did, especially since in my mind, I was racking up points on the Good Husband scale. I was experiencing growth. I was finally doing the right thing. Obviously, I was wrong. Because there I was, trying to figure out how I ended up in my current position. Growth was supposed to be a good thing.

Everyone should have a yearning to grow. However, growth is inevitable, even when it feels like we are not taking part. Growth is always happening. It takes place even when we least expect it to, without our recognition or permission. Growth manifests itself in many forms, even in the lives of couples. Couples can grow up, grow together, or grow apart. The marital relationship should be cultivated so that they grow together.

Have you ever thought about this? When people plant roses, they purposely plant them in boxes because roses tend to grow wild. The box gives the roses space to grow; the growth just takes place within the confinement of the box. I believe this concept should be applied to relationships. A subliminal box should be placed around the relationship, equipped with the necessary space for two people to grow individually and collectively. They should encourage one another to complete personal and individual goals, as well as collective goals, making sure to mark every milestone. They should continue to date one another, encourage one another, doing all they can to make each other happy, as well as foster an environment based on effective communication. The key would be doing it together; they would grow together. Unfortunately, I learned this too late. We both grew; we just made the mistake of not growing together.

Growing together should be the goal. To do this, couples must figure out how to manage their growth. Nikki and I did not excel in this area. At least, I didn't do much that would qualify as "managing" growth. And I have taken responsibility for that. At a certain point, we related vicariously through James, Kennedy, and McKenzie. We had the routine down to a science. We got our children off to school every day. We stressed the importance of education and encouraged them to make good grades. We introduced them to extracurricular activities and allowed them to choose whether they wanted to continue. James chose baseball, Kennedy chose softball, and McKenzie chose cheerleading. These activities were both demanding and expensive. The kids needed team practices, individual lessons, and one-on-one sessions if we were going to achieve our desired results. What results did we want? Notice how I use the terms, we and ours. We were in this together and if we did it right, we would receive our desired results: College scholarships, discipline, comradery, maybe even the MLB. We seemed to be on the right trajectory.

Our son James (Tré) was on a top travel baseball team and was highly ranked at his position. He achieved good grades and was very well mannered. Kennedy played softball well enough to earn a scholarship but was an even better academician. We knew she would be okay. The youngest, McKenzie, was a cheerleader literally and figuratively. She had her own endeavors, but supported her siblings because their schedules were so demanding, and in the process, maintained good grades. The seeds were planted. The plan appeared to be coming together. The children were great and on the path towards greatness. Our investments seemed to be paying off. Little did I know that what I thought were investments would prove to be sacrifices. We were taught in church that a sacrifice is anything that makes you say "ouch." I was hurting, mentally and physically. These were my thoughts. I asked, Why am I thinking these things now?

(These were the thoughts that bombarded the forefront of my thoughts on that Sunday afternoon in October.)

Nevertheless, I continued thinking...

I started to ponder our past few years of marriage. I missed, or ignored, the signs. Nikki and I stopped talking; we just communicated. We still looked the part. We showed up at family functions together, attended worship together, slept in the same bed, and pulled off holiday celebrations-even when it seemed like we wouldn't be able to. God's grace was evident because even in what looked like dysfunction, there appeared to be function. We didn't share much laughter. We just got caught up in the hustle and bustle of parenting. Everything was about our children; very little was about us. Mutual communication was nonexistent.

That was troublesome because society is big on communication and offers multiple ways to do it. We can call, text, email, FaceTime, Duo. We can use Messenger on Facebook. There are many ways to ease communication, but not all of them are effective. For instance, texting, a popular form of communication, can easily be misinterpreted because texts have no tone. Interpretation is left to the reader. Texting removes the intimacy that talking provides. Talking requires a listener. Listening enables one to hear inflections – excitement, sadness – in the speaker's tone. Talking brings an atmosphere of closeness that texting cannot. I remember our texting each other while in the same house. And while we invested time and effort into our children, we neglected our relationship. We rarely dated, something we used to do all the time. When we were younger, we went to an upscale restaurant most weekends. Of course, this was prior to having children. By the end of the marriage, we only went upscale on anniversaries and Valentine's Day. It's sad, I know. She deserved better. No, *we* deserved better, but we fell short and now we are in separate dwelling places, and I was alone, sitting here, stuck on the couch.

In Jeremiah 29:11, God assured the children of Israel that He had their best interests at heart. He had plans to bring them to an expected end. That's good news! Why? It's because God is not a respecter of persons. He's not like us. He doesn't choose favorites; neither does He disregard people because of their pedigree or lack thereof. He has plans and promises for all His children. The problem comes when our circumstances don't match the promises. Therein lies the problem. At the time, my present looked nothing like my promise. It honestly felt like I was stuck in a downward spiral with no end in sight. Have you been there? How did you handle it?

Typically, when we get involved, we have a way of prolonging the process. In all actuality, our best option is inaction.

Really, our only choice is to wait.

Wait? That's hard to do, especially if you find yourself worrying, because worry fuels doubt and doubt does a couple of things. As a filter, worry causes you to look at what is and see only what you want to see. I was divorced but kept seeing us back together. No matter how many times Nikki told me it was over, I refused to accept it. I allowed doubt to cloud my vision. Doubt is a breeding ground for fear, and we already know God did not give us a spirit of fear, but of love, power, and a sound mind. I was literally terrified of facing life on my own.

That's why when life deals you a bad hand, that's not the time to panic or pout. That's the perfect time to pray. Grandmama and "nem" used to say if you call Him and call Him right, He will show up. In those moments of despondency, it may appear that we are alone, but that's a façade. It is a trick of the enemy to make us feel alone, when in actuality, God never left. He is standing at the door of our hearts knocking, waiting for us to let Him in. And when we let Him in, He comes in and removes the scales from our eyes, enabling us to see clearly. Believe me, I'm a witness. Here's the thing. We might not like what He shows us. In fact, we might not even want to see what He is showing us. But trust me, if He is revealing something to us, we need to see it because it is a part of our process. Being stuck on that couch, asking myself how

I ended up here was part of my process; it slowed me down and gave me clearer vision. At this point, my perspective began to change.

Touch your neighbor and say, IT WAS PART OF THE PROCESS!

The Mirror of the Rear

As I sat there on the couch, my mind began to play the blame game with me as its focal point. "Everything is your fault" is what I told myself, and I was finally taking the time to look in the mirror. I know it sounds strange, but over the years, I rarely took the time to look in the mirror. It was my body, and I knew where everything was, so I didn't think looking in the mirror was necessary. I didn't need the mirror to wash my face nor to brush my teeth. I knew the natural grain of my hair, so it was easy to brush it. I usually tied my tie in the car, on the way to my destination. So, looking in the mirror just wasn't a necessity.

But here I was, looking into a metaphorical mirror, focusing on my circumstances, and wondering how I ended up here. The mirror I had ignored was now crystal clear and seemed to reflect images in 3-D. Things that had gone unnoticed suddenly revealed themselves, demanding that I take notice. There was no Windex or Sprayway, but now that I was taking the time to look, the mirror was prepared to reveal some ugly truths. The images played a slideshow of my mistakes of the last 17 years. I was looking in a rearview mirror.

Rearview Mirrors

A rearview mirror is a small, angled mirror fixed inside the windshield of a motor vehicle, enabling the driver to see the vehicle or road behind. Rearview mirrors are made up of two main components, a wedge-shaped mirror and a pane of glass covering that mirror. When the mirror is in its normal position, light rays hit our eyes, allowing us to see what's behind. Somehow, the mirror enables us to see what's behind as vividly as we simultaneously see what's in front. This tiny piece of glass carries a subtle, yet ominous warning: "Objects in mirror are closer than they appear." As I sat there on the couch, I began to reflect on my own rear view.

Certain scenes lit up. I remember saying to myself, if I were her, I would have left me, too. Only I would have done it a long time ago. Because at one time, I wasn't a very good husband. I'm not making excuses, but I was probably not mature enough to get married at the time we got married. Had I allowed hindsight to speak, it probably would have advised me to wait. But I didn't. I proposed, we got married, had a child, and started life together, raising a family. Nikki was light years ahead of me in maturity. I grew up but did so too late. I thought I had grown up in time. Evidently not. So, I began this trip down memory lane and saw some of the mistakes I made, fallout from my bad decisions, unfilled expectations, and lack of achievement. I thought about some of the lies I'd told, the promises I failed to keep, the struggles that never seemed to end. They lined up to present themselves as to why I was here on the couch and not home with my family.

Could it have been for the shattering news that almost broke us up the first time? I never will forget the look on Nikki's face. She was devastated. The world as she knew it had come to a screeching halt. The future she envisioned was in jeopardy because of my selfishness. I sacrificed my family for a feeling that was supposed to be temporary but stretched into 18 years. So, I wouldn't have blamed her had she left. She had every right, and now a good reason, to leave. But she stayed. And what I did then was much worse than what I have done recently. Could it have been for the unsolicited phone calls she neither asked for nor deserved? I was a mess and sometimes things got messy. Let's just say she didn't deserve what she went through. She endured all my antics and that had to weigh heavily on her.

This was ironic because it was probably the first time I found myself doing an honest assessment of my life and didn't like what I saw. I abhorred the man in the mirror. I saw someone who was favored by God and the recipient of a major promise, not living up to expectations. After all, I started preaching in 1994 when I was only 21 years old. When I first received the call to preach, all I wanted to do was study, go to church, and preach. I started preaching at Antioch Full Baptist Church under the leadership of Bishop Kenneth L. Robinson, Sr. He exposed me to some of the nation's greatest preachers. I was fascinated by their minds. I loved how they were able to communicate the gospel through expression. Their vocabularies, vocal abilities, and abilities to connect with large crowds, all these things were fascinating to me. I made up my mind that I wanted to preach for the rest of my life, and I started to make the necessary preparations.

My Call

Before we get into the preparations, let's go back and look at the process that led to my call. In 1993, I was attending the University of Arkansas-Little Rock and a member of White City Memorial Baptist Church, my family's church in which I grew up. I was working two part-time jobs, one as a driver for Pathfinders Daycare and one as a telemarketer for Southwestern Bell. By this time, I had gone off to college and had been exposed to young adults doing church differently. So, I found myself trying to supplement my spirituality beyond what I was receiving at my home church. One day I was listening to local radio KITA and heard Bishop Paul S. Morton was preaching a revival at the then Antioch Baptist Church. He was one of those singing preachers who fascinated me as well. I loved to hear him sing, "Your Tears Are Only Temporary." Well, I went to the revival. That night, he preached a sermon that touched my heart, entitled "The Lost Axe Head." I was so touched that I decided Antioch would be my church home and Kenneth Robinson would be my pastor. My heart was filled with joy. I was comfortable with my decision.

Everything was great until I got home. I was 21 yrs. old at the time and lived with my parents. Anyway, when I shared with my parents that I was changing church homes, the news resulted in an argument. I couldn't believe it; I got fussed at. This was supposed to be one of the happiest days of my life. Instead, I was being ostracized because of my church choice. I think I was accused of only wanting to join so I could sing in the choir. If that was the reason, what was wrong with that? At least, I would be in church serving. Shouldn't that have been the goal? If you train up a child as the Bible teaches, that child will eventually remain true to that training. A parent's job is to lay the foundation for their children and hope they choose according to the teachings they have been exposed to all their lives. I just chose to move my membership to a larger church with more young people my age, with a pastor to whom I could relate, and it didn't hurt that they had an awesome choir. That was a rough night, but we got through it.

Maturity has taught me to look at that whole situation with different lenses, especially since becoming a parent. Some traditions are not easily broken for families. They were used to my attending church with them. I did some of everything at White City. I sang in the choir, served as an usher and junior deacon, and taught Sunday school. I did all these things at different points over the previous 11 or 12 years. That was a tough pill to swallow, but it was time for the baby bird to leave the nest. I was growing up and it was time to make my own decisions. My decision was to join Antioch Baptist Church.

I went on to start serving at Antioch. I attended Sunday services religiously, went to Bible study regularly, and eagerly joined the choir. I was enjoying church like never before. I had not one family member in that church, but I felt at home.

The more I attended Bible study, the more I wanted to learn about God. The more I learned about God, the more I developed a yearning. Growing up, I received the learning, but not this type of burning. Something began to tug on my spirit. I began to have dreams where I saw myself in a pulpit preaching. One day, while driving the van for Pathfinder, I had a minor accident. Thankfully, I had already dropped off the last child when someone rear-ended me in West Little Rock, off Barrow Rd, on the ramp leading to I-630 East. That accident caused me to miss 47 days of work. During those 47 days, every day the church was open, I was there. My dreams intensified. My personal life started to feel very uncomfortable. Nothing seemed to be going right. I was going through a definite life change. I even considered joining the military, but couldn't get a waiver because I am asthmatic.

One Wednesday, after leaving Bible study, I came home and went to bed. That night I had a very intense dream. The enemy came into my bedroom to scare me from completing my assignment. The devil sent imps to remind me of every bad thing I had done. They tried to make me think I was not worthy to preach the gospel. I was going through real life spiritual warfare in my parents' home, while I am sure they were sleeping peacefully.

Things climaxed when I had a vision of myself lying in bed, catatonic, then, being lifted out of my bed. I tried to move but could not. All I was able to do was turn my head. I turned my head towards my Bible and said, "Jesus." At that point, I was lowered back onto the bed and released. I felt a great calm. After the enemy made his attempt, God moved. I literally saw myself in the pulpit preaching my first sermon. Then, I heard God's voice tell me to preach his word. Not long after that, I went to church and shared with my pastor that I had been called to preach. His response was strange: he offered very little encouragement, thinking that if he could discourage me, then the call wasn't genuine. I was persistent. So, he trained me and allowed me to preach my first sermon on February 20, 1994. Now, back to the preparations...

This was a time of transition for Bishop Robinson and our church. Bishop received an invitation to sit on the Council of Bishops for the Full Gospel Baptist Church (FGBC). The FGBC was a movement and fellowship started by Bishop Paul S. Morton, which gave Baptists the "right to choose" if they wanted to operate in the gifts of the Spirit. This caused a significant rift in the body of Christ among Baptists. Anyway, Bishop Robinson was my pastor, and I was there for him during that turbulent time.

I remember being there for his consecration. Well-known preachers came from all over the country, and he introduced me to many of them. I was admitted to certain rooms simply by being associated with Bishop Robinson. He prepared me for ministry by giving me opportunities to teach and preach at our church and by introducing me to and promoting me with other pastors. He also chose me to be State Youth Overseer for the Arkansas FGBC. In fact, I was the first one. My responsibilities included traveling around the state of Arkansas conducting youth revivals. Fellow pastors Stephen T. Robinson, Dwight Townsend, Jason Talbert and I went from church-to-church, tag team preaching. Bishop prepared me for ministry through practical, on-the-job training.

In 1995, Bishop Robinson started the simultaneous revival format in the Little Rock area. Rev. Keith Smith, Rev. E.F. Ledbetter, Rev. Sammie Rash, and a host of others came to our city and ran simultaneous revivals. I remember sitting there in awe as I listened to Keith Smith's powerful preaching. I remember thinking how brilliant he and the other revivalists were and I wanted to do it like that, but how?

I spent a couple of years in college, but I was taking a break and seminary wasn't on my radar. But as fortune would have it, I was working at an alternative school as an in-house suspension (ISS) monitor. When students at the high school got suspended, they had to come to my class and stay until their suspension was complete. In my class, they were not allowed to talk. They were only allowed to do two things: the homework assigned by their teachers and an essay assigned by me. I think it might have been somewhere between 5 and 10 pages. Those were some interesting papers. I read constantly because I was in an environment conducive to reading. I read Matthew Henry,

Watchman Nee, Frank and Ida Hammond, J. Vernon McGee, Max Lucado, and host of others. I knew voracious reading was another way of preparing myself for ministry.

I also figured that as a preacher, I was going to have to get married at some point. So, when I looked at women, I tried to imagine some of them as my wife. I didn't even know what qualities I was looking for; I just figured when I saw her, I would know. I was in no hurry. After all, I was only 21. I had the rest of my life. I just wanted to preach and become pastor of my own church one day.

Prior to working full-time as the ISS monitor, I served as a substitute teacher at the high school. While there, I met a young man a couple of years younger than I, and also a preacher. It so happened that Pastor Jerry Black was running a revival in Pine Bluff. He was well-known because he was from Little Rock, but had moved to Atlanta. So, whenever he came to Arkansas, wherever he would preach, that church would usually be packed. Well, one of those nights, that young preacher and I decided to ride to Pine Bluff to hear Black preach. We passed by a car on the highway, and he started waving at the young lady inside the car. He told me her name was Nikki and said how she loved Pastor Black. He said Pastor Black was the reason she was going to college in Atlanta. I didn't pay much attention to him that day. However, the next day, while subbing at the school, that same young lady walked into one of my classes. I thought she was cute, but she was too young. I think I was 20 and she was 17. Don't quote me on that. Anyway, I didn't say anything to her.

Later that summer, I ran into Nikki at the mall while she was working at a clothing store. This time, I saw her in a different light. She was grown-grown-LOL. We talked; she said she was preparing to go to Spelman College in Atlanta soon. I gave her my card, but she didn't call. That fall semester went by without my hearing from her. But I ran into her again at a church function while she was visiting home. I gave her my card again, but she didn't call-AGAIN. She went back to campus and returned. I ran into her at another church function. I gave her my card again and she still didn't call. This time, I was a little bothered. I thought Nikki was beautiful. She carried herself like a lady. And she had a magnetic smile. But she didn't call. Oh, well. By the time I showed up at church that Sunday morning, she called the church to get in touch with me under the guise of someone wanting me to preach at their church. We exchanged numbers and the rest was the beginning of history. We spent all our available time together that summer. That had to be one of the best summers of my life. All too soon, those days came to an end.

When August came, and it was time for Nikki to go back to school, I was not ready. I think I ran up a $800 cell phone bill trying to maintain contact with her. I called every day. She was gone barely a month before I made plans to go visit. Little did I know that the visit that was supposed to be temporary would turn into me changing my address. I visited on a Friday, got a job on Monday, flew back to Arkansas on Tuesday, and moved to Atlanta, Georgia on Wednesday. I left everything- family and friends. I didn't even say goodbye. I just left. But I didn't look at it as leaving. I looked at it as going. I was going to a place that would offer better opportunities, but more than anything, I could be with the woman with whom I had fallen in love. After all, I felt like Nikki was destined to be my wife.

Nikki had all the qualities: 5 ft 3" tall, small frame, dark-skinned, smart, ladylike, and saved. She knew and loved the Lord: profile of the perfect preacher's wife. I was determined to be with her and was not going to let go. I relocated, moved to Georgia and got in the car business. I found a newspaper ad where they were hiring salespeople at a Mitsubishi dealership in Duluth, GA. I didn't know it was 45 minutes across town. I just went to the interview and got the job.

At the time, Nikki's parents didn't know that I had left Little Rock and relocated to Georgia, and I was determined to be in my own apartment before they found out. When I first moved, I stayed with Nikki and her roommates. That was when I realized how much she loved me. When I left Little Rock, I had $118 and a trunk full of clothes in plastic bags. She took my clothes out of those bags, folded and organized them, and welcomed me into her home. We spent all our time together. If I wasn't at work and she wasn't at school, we were together, going to nice restaurants, going to church, and just hanging out.

I stayed with them for approximately a month and a half until I got my second paycheck. Then, I moved into a one-bedroom apartment in Lithia Springs. I loved my apartment: It had a garden tub in the bathroom, French doors in the bedroom, a fireplace, and a spacious balcony. Life seemed to be going in the right direction.

After living in Atlanta for about a year-and-a-half, I joined the Elizabeth Baptist Church (EBC), under the leadership of Pastor Craig Oliver. Prior to that I served at Hunter Hill but decided to leave to be a part of the EBC ministry. It was progressive. They had just built a beautiful church. The choirs were good, the atmosphere was vibrant, and the pastor was dynamic. Ironically, he was younger than I, but was one of the best preachers I ever heard. He was very disciplined when it came to reading. He encouraged us to study, and would borderline embarrass us if we didn't. I was eager to join the church and learn from Rev. Oliver. Nikki and I both joined and embraced the culture of the church. Pastor O gave me plenty of opportunities. I led Call to Worship pretty much every week. I taught Bible study. I preached whenever I was given the chance. And I got a lot of engagements because of my association with Elizabeth. I would be gone from EBC for months at a time preaching at different churches. I was really being prepared for ministry. Pastor Oliver made sure of that.

In January 1998, Nikki and I got married in the chapel of EBC, with Pastor Oliver as the officiant. It finally happened. She was my wife. Reality had set in. We had officially changed her last name. The process was complete, and I was scared as h*@#! Was I ready? Would I live up to her expectations? What kind of husband would I be? Would we be good as pastor and first lady? Did I even want to get married? These were some of the questions that crossed my mind. Well, I couldn't worry about that anymore because the deed was done.

We didn't wait. We started a family right away. God blessed us with a baby boy on July 18, 1998. Nikki's mother swore up and down it would be a girl, but I told her it would be a boy. At 2:26 a.m., at Parkway Medical Center, James Henry Kirklin III, whom we nicknamed Tré, made his entrance into the world. At the time, we were living in a two-bedroom apartment in Austell. I was working in the car business, and she was working at the same hospital where she gave birth. We lived there three years before buying our first home, a 4-bedroom, 2-story home in Powder Springs. It was in a nice quiet subdivision and had a fenced-in backyard, the perfect home. Things were going well. I had received a promotion on my job. Nikki had graduated from Spelman College and was doing well. We were on the right trajectory. At least, I thought we were.

But here was the problem. I lived one way publicly but a different life privately. The car business is something else. It will expose a person to different types of spirits and if he is not disciplined, he can easily be sucked in. I was 26 years old, making good money, and doing everything I wanted to do. I had the Midas touch;

everything I touched was turning into gold. I mean, less than 6 years ago, I came to Atlanta with $118 in my pocket and a trunk full of clothes. Now, we were living in a four-bedroom home. I had a beautiful wife and a wonderful son. Not long after buying the house, I put a Mercedes in the driveway for Nikki. All that looked good on the surface. No "trouble in Paradise" here. We looked like a TV family; put on a good show for the neighborhood.

We humans are dichotomous; we have equally strong spiritual sides and natural sides. The challenge is to keep the flesh under subjection. If we allow the flesh to rise, the flesh will dominate and lead us to make bad decisions. I admit that I allowed my flesh to rise, and I made some very unwise decisions, not realizing that those decisions would have lasting ramifications. That's why Peter told the early church in his first epistle that they should remain sober and vigilant at the same time, because the enemy is equivalent to a roaring lion seeking someone to devour (I Peter 5:8). Lack of soberness can cause one to forego one's own morality. My choices did not lead to good outcomes; they shattered trust, created enmity, and jeopardized my marriage.

Like the time I went to a party and had a drink far later than I should have, waiting for "the saints" to leave. Well, a police officer pulled me over on my way home. My stomach dropped when I saw those blue lights in my rearview mirror. Here I was, a preacher, getting a DUI. Now let me acknowledge, I was not drunk. I was a Black man driving a brand, new Mercedes Benz in Cobb County, Georgia, at 2 in the morning. A good husband would have been home in bed with his wife, instead of in "the streets," placing himself in danger. That's just one stupid thing I did that could have jeopardized our marriage.

In retrospect, maybe God was trying to warn me. Like the time I was in that club that I had no business being in and ran into a church member. Neither of us had any business being there, especially me. Not only was I married, but I was also a minister at a megachurch with thousands of members whose eyes were on me weekly. I took a huge risk by being there and I was caught red-handed. I had to come up with a plan quick. I didn't want to get outed by a member who had something on me. I remember saying to myself that I was going to put him in a position where he couldn't tell. I made sure he had the time of his life. We both had a really good time. If my 49-year-old self would have been in that same position, I guarantee you I would never have gone to that place again. But the 27 year-old me might have gone back the next week. That's sad. I know. God was giving me chance after chance, and I ignored the signs.

In the few years that followed, I subtly put my wife through a lot. Somewhere along the way, I became a functioning alcoholic. I was never diagnosed or anything, but all I know is that when I drank, my behavior changed. I was mean, arrogant, and stupid. I made a decision that drastically affected my marriage. I had an affair, which resulted in another child. Naturally and expectedly, Nikki took it very hard. The man in whom she had put her trust, to have and to hold until death did us part, had betrayed the vows and the marriage. Not only that, but the affair had produced a child. Yes, she was devastated. She should have been.

Few people knew it, but Nikki and I were separated for a couple of months. That was a tough time. We owned a four-bedroom house, but I was living house to house. Thankfully, I had a praying mother-in-law and a wife who knew and recognized the voice of the Lord. Before making the decision to leave me, Nikki spoke with her mother and was asked a very important question. Her mother asked her if she had prayed, and her response was no. Therefore, not long afterwards, she invited me back home. Man, she loved me.

The day I returned home, she had the living room set up like a party. There were banners on the walls, balloons littered the room, and if memory serves me correctly, a cake. Our son was too young to realize what was going on, but he enjoyed the festivities. Everything was perfect. Then, my ex performed one of the greatest acts of forgiveness I've ever seen. She told me that with her, my slate was clean. Despite all I had done, she was willing to cast my transgressions in the sea of forgetfulness. That was amazing! Especially, considering all that I had done. She had every right to walk away and never look back. Thank God she saw the God in me and recognized and respected the call on my life. She probably believed in me more than I believed in myself. Because had I believed in myself, I probably wouldn't have done anything to mar that clean slate. But over the years, I did. I continued the affair. To be honest, I remember tricking myself into believing I could be happy in either situation. Listen...be careful when entertaining conversations with the enemy. His mission is to disrupt God's plan for your life. Don't do what I did. I supplied the ammunition the enemy was using to kill me, and if he was killing me, he was also killing us.

Perhaps, this was the reason I was in my current position, stuck here on the couch. Maybe, Nikki got tired and wanted to preserve a part of her youth. These were thoughts I was thinking for her, justifying why she left me. She could have left, but she hung in there. And what did she get in return? More years of heartache. I say that sarcastically because although we experienced "heartache," for some reason, we were insulated. We went through fire but didn't smell like smoke. We almost drowned a few times but felt no remnants from the water. Although we struggled, I always felt like we were struggling to, not through. My feelings were that God was using our struggle as a lesson for others (I still believe that). But I guess she got tired...understandably and deservedly so.

Or perhaps it was for the bad financial decisions I made. It is hard operating from a platform of struggle and survival, but that's what we did. It didn't have to be that way. When you are running as a shell of a man, you might find yourself reacting instead of dictating. As life happened, at a certain point, we became the casualty of it. Bills, fees, and responsibilities kept coming. Between those blue lights and that bad decision, I became broken and battered. Nevertheless, I had to wear those masks. I had to be able to switch seamlessly at a moment's notice. I had to be husband, father, minister, co-worker, and overall citizen in the community. Not that that's any more than anyone else does, I just did it while broken and battered. I remember working a job that I hated, and it was almost two months before I realized I wasn't making any money. It was hard to see the reflection in the mirror when I was looking with a blind mind like the one Paul spoke of to the Corinthian church. The god of this world blinds the minds of the lost, preventing the light of the gospel to shine like it should.

Shut off notices, penalties, and late fees were the norm. Payments were late. Nikki hated that. On numerous occasions, she told me security was her love language. I heard her, but I'm not sure if I was really listening. I got a little better, but I'm not sure if I really changed. Maybe that was the reason. Who knows?

Perhaps it was the trajectory our lives had taken. I thought for sure by now, I would have been the pastor of a church, traveling around the country preaching and teaching the word of God. My experiences include serving on staff at a couple of large churches in Metro Atlanta. In those settings, I was constantly told that my time was coming, that I should just be patient. Year after year, I sent resumes to churches all over the country, to no avail.

I think I came in second about seven times. I never admitted it, but that affected my psyche. I won't say it broke me, but I know it fractured my confidence. I settled into my role as husband and father supporting my children in their endeavors. The commitment we made to baseball and softball demanded so much of our time. There were many Sundays that I was not at church because I was at the baseball field. But I never stopped preaching, hoping for that one opportunity that never came. I wonder if that made Nikki see me differently, as "less than."

Whatever it was has me here, stuck on this couch, on the verge of divorce after almost 20 years of marriage, facing the reflections in this mirror. And to be honest, I despised the reflection looking back at me. Who had I become? I was no longer in the house to support and protect my family. Things were changing drastically; my only option was to adjust to those changes. What a scary sight!

In instances like these, it is important that we remember both who we are and Whose we are. Self-talk, when infiltrated by the enemy, can be dangerous and detrimental because it encourages us to doubt ourselves. It might be noble to shoulder the responsibility and take all the blame for the shortcomings in a relationship. But truthfully, that is too much weight for one person to bear. For whatever reason, relationships fail. We must not view failure as final. Instead, we should view that as a steppingstone instead of a stop sign. It's time to traverse the rearview. Get out of the mud, get off the couch and move forward.

The Conversations We Should Have Had

I remember as if it were yesterday. It was a normal, family evening like any other; home from work, home from school. Kennedy and McKenzie were in their respective rooms. Nikki was in her usual position, sitting in bed working and watching TV. I was downstairs, lying on the same couch on which I am now stuck. Nikki sent a text asking me to come upstairs. I had no idea what she wanted. I walked up the stairs, around the corner into the bedroom, and stood at the foot of the bed. I was not at all ready for the next words that came out of her mouth, words that would alter my present reality. She spoke. "James, I found a rental. The girls and I are moving out." I stood there in shock - literally numb. I could not believe she was saying these words. She waited for a response, but honestly, I didn't have one. She asked, "Do you want to talk about it?" My reply was, "There's nothing I can say. You've obviously made up your mind." I went downstairs and flopped down on the couch. This time, however, I didn't go to sleep. I started thinking.

My thoughts racing, I began to remember clues that I missed in the past. One of the girls would say they went house shopping while I was at work. I thought they were going house shopping for us, not just for them. I guess I could have asked. And had I asked, what answer would I have received? Would I have thrown a monkey wrench in Nikki's plan? After all, our conversations were very limited back then; most were done vicariously through the children. But I know one thing about her; she was not going to leave haphazardly. That plan had to be in the works for months, if not years. I imagine it even took a lot of courage for her to utter those fateful words.

I wrestled with these thoughts while lying on that couch. In hindsight, I should not have sat on the couch wondering. Instead, I should have been upstairs asking for answers. And while I'm here in my new place reflecting on that awful night, I think about the conversation we should have had. In scenario #1, I can imagine the conversation going like this:

Nikki: "James, I found a rental. The girls and I are moving out."

Me: "Huh?"

Nikki: "You heard me. I found a rental. We're leaving."

Me: "I'm confused. Why?"

Nikki: "C'mon, Henry (She is the ONLY one who calls me Henry), you know we haven't been happy in a long time."

Me: "Speak for yourself. I'm happy."

Nikki: "Well, I'm not happy and haven't been in a long time.

I would have asked what it was that I did specifically that made her come to this decision at this time, but I was afraid of the answer. In fact, I thought I already knew. After all, I had caused much harm, and most of it made me a worthy candidate to be left. I had done some egregious things, things that a married man has no business doing. And here I was on the cusp of a separation. Instead of staying downstairs, I should have gone back upstairs and asked another question:

Me: "After 19 years, why now?"

Nikki: "How much longer would you prefer I wait?"

(I imagine right about now she would have launched into a soliloquy.)

Nikki: "I've been waiting for almost 20 years. Year after year, the kids and I have been the casualties of your bad decisions. I have waited – you know I have – hoping things would change, but they haven't."

(Honestly, I would have understood what she was saying, but I also knew I had made a lot of positive strides. So, that was my only comeback.)

Me: "But, I have changed. My desires have changed. I come home every night."

(I probably had an eerie semblance of a gospel quartet singer.)

"The things that I used to do, I don't do any more. The places I used to go, I don't go to those places anymore."

Nikki: "I'm sorry, but it's too late." This isn't the first time you have done better." It's a part of your pattern. You change for a while and then you revert to the behaviors of your past. I can't take that chance any longer."

Me: "But, I'm grown now."

I really was. In my eyes, I had finally grown up. I had grown into the man I needed to be for my family, and I was working on being a better husband for my wife. Trust me. I knew my shortcomings.

Nikki: It's too late.

At that point, I imagine I would have walked away in defeat. But at least, I would have fought. I would have put up the imagery that my family was worth fighting for. Instead, I tucked my tail between my legs and headed downstairs, sulking in sorrow. Part of me pondered the possibilities of being single. All the things that marriage restricted, being single would give me the freedom to do. If I wanted to be with multiple women, I could. If I wanted to stay in the house all day and not be bothered, I would be able to. I seriously considered those options. Then, another part of me was terrified. I was used to this life. I had settled into certain norms. I had specific expectations. I had to maintain routines. For instance, I knew where we would spend Thanksgiving. I was used to waking up on Christmas morning and watching James, Kennedy, and McKenzie open their gifts. We had created a culture, but all that was now in jeopardy because of a decision *she* made. And I couldn't help but wonder, why didn't she do this a long time ago? It would have made sense if she had done it then. It just didn't make sense to me. Who was in her ear? Who was she getting advice from? How would she survive alone if we were struggling together? These questions flooded my mind as I went back downstairs and slept on the couch.

In scenario #2, the conversation could have gone like this:

Nikki: "I found a rental, and the girls and I are moving out."

Me: What? No... Why? Please don't leave me. I can't make it on my own. I need you.

I imagine she probably would have started crying. With tears running down her face, she probably would have said:

Nikki: "No, James; I have tried time after time and year after year. I have to do this for me."

Me: "Nooooo, Baby…. My destiny is tied up in you. Remember, we're on a mission for the kingdom. We haven't been struggling through, we have been struggling 'to.' We're almost there. Don't give up."

Nikki: "For how long though? How long do we have to suffer? How long do I have to put up with your bad decisions? I'm tired. I feel like I need to break away and be on my own."

Me: "If you can find it in your heart to give me one more chance, please do. I promise I won't mess this up. I tell you what. Pray about it."

I would not have made that challenge if I didn't feel as if God wouldn't stop the divorce and change her mind.

In this scenario, she would have reluctantly given me another chance. If this had happened, I wouldn't be here stuck on the couch. Instead, I would be in the same house as my family, sleeping in the same bed as the person I said that I would be with for better or worse, in sickness and in health, until death did us part. I guess this was true because the relationship was undoubtedly dying.

Although we didn't have either of the conversations mentioned in the two scenarios, I experienced the results of the first conversation. I was unable to change her mind. Those were conversations that we didn't have, but over the next couple of months we did have at least one more conversation because she didn't leave right away. We never argued, so the atmosphere was amicable. We slept in the same bed, ate at the same table, rode in the same car, and attended the same events. We got along fine. In fact, things were so normal that I was hoping she would change her mind. A part of me had made up my mind that wherever they were going, I was going, too. I still had not wrapped my mind around living life without my family.

I remember one incident quite vividly. It was Sunday morning, and I was scheduled to preach at a church searching for a pastor. Even though our marriage was on the rocks, in my mind we were still together, so I took my family with me. Presenting them, more specifically Nikki, knowing we might not be together may have been a mistake. She was anointed and attractive with an infectious smile. I knew the members would be drawn to her. In fact, a member of a search committee at a church in Florida told me that Nikki was my "secret weapon." On this day, she introduced herself to me before I spoke. I don't think she had a problem with James, the preacher. She had a problem with James, the husband. And when she introduced me, she introduced the preacher. The congregation fell in love with her. The Lord let me say it pretty good that day, so the congregation was excited about my family and me. I was on a spiritual high. We rode home as a family, went to dinner, and went home as if everything was normal. But when I look at it in hindsight, she spent the majority of that afternoon outside the house. I later learned that she was preparing to move to her new home-the one that did not include me.

Later that night, Nikki called with a message that shattered my world again. She said it was time to tell the kids we would be separating. My mind was so jumbled. I knew it was coming, but I had swept it under the rug. Especially today, after experiencing that congregation and their spirited response, I just knew it was worth waiting to see if anything would materialize. But no, she had made up her mind. She was ready to go and there was nothing I could say or do that would change her mind.

I remember the conversation well. Along with our daughters Kennedy and McKenzie, we sat in the living room, and called Tre on speakerphone because he was away at college. The scene was set. Everyone was in their respective places. Kennedy was sitting on the floor. McKenzie was standing. I think I might have been sitting on the couch and Mom, Nikki, was sitting in the armchair. Once again, our son was on the phone. She started the conversation like this:

Nikki: *"We need to talk to you all. Your dad and I are going to be splitting up. We're still Team Kirklin, we just won't be living in the same house. Nothing else will change."*

The older two took it very well. They only seemed to be concerned about their mom's happiness. If she was unhappy, then she should seek happiness. That seemed to be their attitude. Tré, speaking in 3rd person, said, *"It's like Dad did something to hurt Mom a long time ago and she never got over it."* Kennedy said, *"Mom, if you're unhappy, you have to do what you have to do to find happiness."*

I remember thinking, What about my happiness? Men are expected to be strong and unaffected by circumstances. Everyone was concerned about her happiness, but no one was concerned about my mental well-being. After all, I was the man in the situation. I was expected to be tough, resilient. Little did any of them know my mental state; I am not sure if they were even concerned.

McKenzie, the baby, took it a little harder. For some reason, she assumed the blame for the divorce. When her mom tried to reassure her that nothing would change, her response was, *"But, we won't be living in the same house."*

Then she proceeded to cry. That messed me up. Because I didn't want a divorce. After all, I had grown up. I had finally changed for what I thought was the better.

We assured her that it had nothing to do with her by explaining that we had just grown apart. We still loved each other but things had changed, and no, we weren't going to be living in the same house.

Shortly after that, they started moving things from this house to the new house - clothes, beds, household items - they started moving those things to THEIR new house. Reality was setting in. I didn't know what I was going to do. I started to panic because I didn't have a plan. Mentally, I wandered aimlessly. I worked a job that I hated just to satisfy Nikki. So, I wasn't really making much money. I was doing okay, but I was certainly not living up to my potential. I had no clue what I was going to do. I contemplated going back to Arkansas. But what would I look like as a 45-year-old man moving back home with his parents? I didn't really have any friends that I was close to, so moving in with someone was not an option. Besides, I didn't think I could do the roommate thing anyway. So, I started one more conversation, one list ditch effort to salvage our marriage. I caught her in the master bedroom closet, put both my hands on her shoulders and looked her in the eyes and asked her for one more chance:

Me (with tears in my eyes): "Listen, don't leave me. Please give me another chance."

Nikki: "I'm moving on."

Me: "But, why leave me now? I'm who you need me to be now. I've grown up. I don't have the same desires. I love you and I love my family. Please don't leave."

Nikki: "James, we're done. I'm moving on."

Me: "But, why?"

Her response blew me away and hammered what little self-esteem I had left. My heart sank to my stomach.

Nikki: "I'm not in love with you, I've lost respect for you, and I don't trust you."

I was speechless. I was hurt because I'd let so many people down. First, I let Nikki down. Secondly, I let my children down. Thirdly, I let our extended family down. Additionally, I let the church community down. And more than anything or anyone, I let myself down. It is often said that that which is done in the dark will eventually come to the light. The light was shining brightly on my life right now and I was about to be exposed. I was about to be a divorced preacher. That was a tough pill to swallow. I was a man who had made a living with his mouth, by being able to talk myself in and out of situations. Unfortunately, this was one situation I could not talk myself out of. She was determined. Her mind was made up. Nikki, my wife, was moving on without me and I had no choice but to accept it.

If a young couple were to ask for a key to making their marriage work, I would encourage them to never stop talking. We used to have a saying in high school; "Conversation rules the nation." Well, conversation might not rule the nation, but it helps develop intimacy. It lets your mate know what you're thinking. It helps to share ideas. Even disagreements are good because they allow you to make up. But a dangerous pattern develops when couples stop talking. Once you stop talking, you start wondering what your partner is thinking. What if their or your assumption is wrong? Now you are angry or have allowed your stress level to rise based on an incorrect assumption. A simple conversation could clear up a lot of unnecessary confusion. Self-talk is a habit that you don't want to allow your spouse to develop. The enemy uses those moments as the perfect opportunity to invade that conversation. And when he does, he usually inserts a seed of doubt. It is in the moments of self-talk when a spouse starts to doubt herself and develop feelings of inadequacy. Clear communication can reduce the impact of those red flags. Lack of communication is the breeding ground for potential problems.

I think at a certain point, Nikki and I developed our own language, but we weren't really communicating. We shared schedules through text messages. We slept in the same bed and watched TV together from time to time. We took part in the children's activities. In fact, the majority of what we did was for our kids. If it wasn't baseball practice, it was a baseball game. If it wasn't softball practice, it was a softball game. If it wasn't driving from tumbling lessons, it was driving from cheerleading competitions. We navigated their schedules like a well-oiled machine. But as efficiently as we ran our house, we struggled in our relationship. In fact, I think she had given up years ago, while I ran under the assumption that things would eventually get better. I should have told her. Those were conversations we should have had.

If I were having a conversation with men contemplating marriage, I would tell them to make communication their number one priority. I would tell them to have a vision for their family and to make sure to articulate that vision to his wife first and then to the rest of his family. She is the perfect ally to help implement the vision for the house. Besides, she wants to and deserves to be a part of the process. As the leader of the house, take the advice of the prophet, Habakkuk, to write the vision and make it plain (Hab 2:2). The vision should be kept at the forefront of the family, so everyone knows their part in the vision. My mistake was, I knew where I was going and navigated for us instead of including her/them in the process. Women don't like to follow blindly, especially if their love language includes security.

Another thing I would encourage them to do is to properly manage the growth. You're going to grow anyway. So, make sure that you manage it right. Many times, we make the mistake of letting a relationship grow in its own direction. Doing so could cause you to grow in different directions, to grow apart instead of together, which should always be the goal. I was the leader of my home, so it was my responsibility to make sure these things happened. I didn't, and it cost me my family. All I had to do was have the right conversations.

The Mirror Becomes Meaningful

"The moment the mirror does not recognize us in anymore, the cards are no longer in our hands. In effect, we have failed to see to the bottom line of our life story and lost our identity."

- Erik Pevernagie

Reality check.

I have finally hit rock bottom.

I have officially lost my way.

Who had I become? So many people had high hopes for me, some even higher than I had for myself. Teachers spoke highly of me. Pastors believed I was destined for greatness. I always felt as if I were going to be rich; I just never knew how. My cognitive skills have always been on point, so when I dream, I dream big. I have always seen myself in a much better position than the one I was currently in. However, at a certain point, my cognitive abilities must have gotten clogged, because I no longer saw myself in a better position. All I saw was my now, and now eerily resembled a nightmare. I had exhausted my human ingenuity. The Midas touch I once owned had now turned to mud. What was I supposed to do? My dad taught me that a man must always keep control. Unfortunately, I didn't take daddy's advice. I lost control, and my life would never be the same.

The first few months in my new place were like "the best of times and the worst of times." I was getting accustomed to a new place, new lifestyle, and new job. At least, I had my job. Well, I thought I did. The day after I moved into my apartment, I went to work and got fired. Go figure. The company had the nerve to fire me. It wasn't like I wasn't being productive. I was selling cars. I really didn't like the job, but I was selling cars. I needed a job because I was going through a divorce and was going to have to get used to paying bills by myself. But check out the reason they fired me: because I didn't smile enough. Would you smile if you were going through an unsolicited divorce?

I remember this one scene where I was literally begging for my job, asking the manager not to fire me. Then I heard the audible voice of the Holy Spirit say, Shut up and leave. I heard it so intently that it almost scared me. I acknowledged that voice by standing up, shaking my manager's hand, and walking out. His confused look told me he wouldn't understand my peace even if I told him.

That was Halloween, 2017. I remember going home and sitting on my couch, trying to figure out how I was going to pay my bills. All I remember is telling myself that I would NEVER again place myself in a position where a person would have the power to fire me.

Now, I'm separated. I don't have the safety net of a spouse and her salary. If I don't pay my rent, I will be evicted. And I don't have a job. Not to mention the three children whose care I share. I had no clue what I was going to do. I knew what I was not going to do; I was not going to work anywhere where someone had the power to fire me. So, I stayed there, stuck on the couch.

The end of the month was coming and I did not have next month's rent. Couple that with the fact that I needed to continue to help Nikki take care of our children. I applied for unemployment, but that wasn't enough to pay rent. If I saved every dime during the month, it wouldn't be enough. I had no source of income. Thankfully, towards the end of the month, a friend called and asked if I was working. I told him that I was not. He said to hold on, that he would call me back in a few minutes. When he called back, he said to pack a bag for 3 days and watch for the Uber driver he was sending to pick me up. Then, I would meet a gentleman named David that I would be working with for the next three days. We would work in Lineville, Alabama, at a small car dealership. They booked David and me into the EconoLodge in Oxford, Alabama (Talk about being in a low place).

David and I worked the first day, but it started snowing profusely the next morning. That was strange, considering we were working in Alabama where it doesn't snow that often. The dealership closed because of the weather, so David and I drove back to Atlanta. He dropped me off and went to his home in North Carolina. Because of the way the week worked out, David was unable to come back to Georgia, so I was paid extra to finish the job. By the time they totaled my earnings, I had enough to pay rent and child support. This verse kept playing in my mind, "Now unto Him who is able to keep us from falling..." (Jude 24a). It was as if God refused to let me fall. Every time I needed Him, He showed up, usually in the form of a phone call. Because the next month I received a similar phone call and received enough money to pay my rent, child support, and have a little change leftover. I knew this was God's way of showing me that He had not forgotten me and that He would supply all my needs if I kept recognizing Him as my source. These were times of transition.

The next couple of years were not only transitional, they were also tumultuous. Life was a rollercoaster, lots of ups and downs, some more taxing than others. Every time I thought I was about to get ahead, something would happen, and I would take several steps backwards. I was a permanent resident somewhere between "Barely Get Along Boulevard" and "Enough Avenue." My days were filled with either fruitfulness or frustration. When I worked, I made enough to support my lifestyle. When I didn't work, I was okay, but I was treading water. I wasn't losing ground, but I wasn't making any progress either. That was not a good foundation for preparation or maintenance during perilous times. And I needed to prepare for my impending future. It was not a smart formula for saving. So, when lean times came, I suffered. That was my fault. Nevertheless, I survived. I suffered, but I survived.

One specific occasion comes to mind. For work, I traveled either to Fort Smith or Fayetteville, Arkansas. The amount of money I was slated to make would cover my bills, but that would be it. There wouldn't be much left over. So, I got paid, paid my bills, and went to my parents' home in Scott, a rural area on the outskirts of North Little Rock. I arrived Saturday night after making the three-hour drive from northwest Arkansas. Whenever I arrived on a Saturday night, the custom was for me to attend church on Sunday and leave Monday. But, when Monday came, I didn't leave. Tuesday came and I didn't leave. Why? Because I was stuck. I had a choice. I could be "broke" in Arkansas or be broke in Atlanta. Talk about tumultuous, "worst of" times. To be honest, I don't think my parents knew I was stuck. They didn't know that I didn't have gas money to get home. So, I had a choice. The man in the mirror was looking at me and I did not like the reflection. He was a very tough pill to swallow.

> *"If you're searching for that one person who will change your life.... take a look in the mirror." - Unknown*

This quote speaks volumes to me. If my life was going to change, I was going to have to take 100% responsibility. Neither individuals nor circumstances could affect me adversely more than I could myself. So, I had to make a conscious decision. Beside my parents' home is a lake. On that Tuesday morning, I walked over and admired the beauty of that lake and asked God to help me get home.

Throughout this marriage pilgrimage, God sent ravens to sustain us, much as he did for Elijah at the Brook of Cherith. In biblical history, God spoke to the prophet Elijah, and after hearing from God, Elijah prophesied to Ahab and Jezebel that no rain would fall from Heaven's celestial faucet until he uttered the word. Because no rain fell, the Earth was forced to endure a severe drought. Imagine those ramifications. No rain, no crops. No crops, no food. Even the stored supply ran out because it could not be replenished. Of course, that would lead to a drought. Because Elijah had prophesied bad news to the king, they put a bounty on his head, commanding that he be killed and causing him to relocate to the Brook of Cherith. Imagine there being a drought everywhere else in the land except for where Elijah was. Elijah made his residence by a brook that kept running despite what was occurring elsewhere in the land. Therefore, Elijah had water to drink. Not only that, each day God reversed the nature of carnivorous birds and instructed them to deliver meat to Elijah. God sustained Elijah because of his obedience; Elijah did what he was told to do. Two miracles stand out:

1. No rain fell, therefore lakes, rivers, and brooks dried up. Water levels dropped daily. However, water never stopped flowing into the brook where Elijah lived. One miracle.
2. Ravens are carnivorous. If they have meat in their mouth, it's usually for consumption. Yet they managed to refrain from eating the

meat and bread they carried to Elijah. That, too, was a miracle.

While I was stuck in Arkansas, God sent one of several ravens. I shared my plight with a friend and before we got off the phone, he Cash-apped me $200 and told me to get home. The next day, I hugged my mom, dapped up my dad, filled up my tank, and hit the road. I got home with less than $100. Rather than feeling sorry for myself, I remembered that I had signed up to do rideshare for Lyft. I made sure my credentials were in order, and the next morning got up, filled up the tank, and turned on my Lyft app. By the end of the day, I had made $150.

Lyft has a feature that enables drivers to access their money daily for a small fee. The next day, I repeated the same process. I woke up, topped off the tank with about $20, and turned on the app again. That day, I made over $200. I cashed out again. The third day was Sunday. I topped off the tank again and turned on the app. Boom! Ding! I received my first run of the day. It was right around the corner, and the caller needed to go to the airport to catch a flight. That day consisted of a lot of long runs. I would drive from Hartsfield-Jackson Airport to Gwinnett County, from Roswell back to the airport, from the airport to Kennesaw. Those were considered long runs. By the end of the day, I had made over $300. Lord knows I needed it. For the first time in a long time, my life was not contingent on what somebody else did for me. If no one called me to work at a dealership, I could still make money and do it daily. I didn't have to worry about my life being adversely affected because of spats with other individuals, of which I seemed to be the only casualty. It was less than what I was used to, but it was enough to take care of my needs and expenses.

Lyfting was my new venture and I got it down to my own perfect science. Lyft usually gave bonuses for consecutive trips during rush hour traffic. For instance, if drivers drove five consecutive trips before 9 A.M., while starting before 7 A.M., the driver would receive a bonus. So, I would wake up about 6:30, leave the house and work the morning shift, ensuring I got all my bonuses. Those hours were usually between 6:45 A.M. and 11 A.M. After that, I would come home, eat lunch, take a nap, and get back out about 2:30 and work the evening rush hour traffic until about 7. That would usually put at least $200 to $250 a day in my pocket. Additionally, Lyft gave bonuses for a specific number of trips. For instance, I might receive an extra $150 for driving 75 trips. Add that to the amount I made daily, and the bills got paid. I did this for a few months until dealership opportunities opened back up.

It has often been said that trials make you strong. If that's the case, I must be Hercules because my trials were coming in waves. If it wasn't one thing, it was another. The next reality check came in the form of the divorce proceeding. The sheriff's department caught me slipping. They knocked on the door and I answered. I was finally served with papers. I say finally, because this was not the sheriff's first visit. They left notices before. But I deceived myself into believing the divorce wasn't official until I accepted the paperwork. I'm not going to lie. Once, I Googled the reference number to find out what the package was. Divorce was inevitable. It didn't matter if I didn't want it; Nikki did. So, it didn't make sense to contest. I made up my mind that I was not going to fight her. Whatever she said she wanted, I would give. After all, she was a good wife. She bore me three children. Why wouldn't I give her whatever she asked, within reason? If I owned the world, I probably would have given her 75% and lived off the rest. I was hoping that absence would make the heart grow fonder, but it didn't. Reconciliation was not to be, and I needed to embrace that. As much as I detested driving, working for Lyft was therapeutic because it helped me deal with these daily trials. I could listen to music, meet new people, and think. Sometimes I felt like a therapist. I was not the only one dealing with personal issues. It seemed as if everyone had their fair share of problems. So, I learned to become empathetic, listening to the problems of others. To an extent, it helped me forget my own issues. I could forget all I wanted to, but this was really happening. And in January of 2019, it was official. It was finally over. We were divorced.

Ironically, not long after this, opportunities started coming again. God knew I needed respite. I wasn't like King David, asking for dove's wings to escape my problem., although I could have used an escape, considering everything that I was going through. So, He allowed the road to be my hiding place. I found myself working in cities I had never visited, such as Roswell, New Mexico; Longview, Texas; Leesburg, Florida; and Germantown, Maryland, to name a few. This was all new to me. I had settled into a comfort zone, but to be successful, I would have to come out of it.

I found myself having to grow up. Many times, I would be on the road three weeks out of the month, which means I slept in a slew of hotel beds, drove numerous rental cars, and ate in countless restaurants. I was happy, because now I was having sustained success. I didn't feel like I was treading water. I was making progress. My life was changing for the better and I was in control.

"Everybody else needs mirrors to remind themselves who they are.

You're no different."

-Jonathan Nolan

Epiphany!

For the first time in a long time, I was paying attention to details. I realized that I didn't have to look in the mirror, but the mirror certainly served its purpose. It revealed things I genuinely needed to see. Had I not seen them, I could not have made the corrections.

I've heard it said that the biggest room in any house is the room for improvement. In my house, that room needed a massive overhaul. The first step of my overhaul included paying my bills on time. Money enabled me to do that, and I had access to money for the first time in a long while. Child support plus everything else my children needed, I could provide. I was able to attend baseball games and softball games. I could go to as many football games to watch my baby girl cheer, because the games were on Friday, and I usually worked between Thursdays and Sundays. The life I should have been living as a husband, I was now living as a single man.

> *"...we went through fire and through water: but thou broughtest us out into a wealthy place."*
> *-Psalm 66:12b*

Finally, my life was meaningful. I was regaining Nikki's respect, and I could see the joy in my children's faces as I was able to supply better. Make no mistake; they never complained. They just adjusted. I put them through so much. Homelessness (although I don't think they realized it), subliminal public scrutiny, a certain degree of lack, among other things. They never judged me. They never stopped loving me. I can't lie. There was a time I felt like they abandoned me.

As a family, I felt like they aborted the mission. They went on with their lives. Forget about dear old dad. Nothing really changed for them. They stayed in the same schools, kept the same habits, still ate fish and spaghetti on Friday night. I was the one who was left alone in silence, with my conscience. But thankfully, I did not succumb to the negative images I set up for myself. Truthfully, the only enemy I had was myself. Living and surviving on the road made me grow up fast. I didn't have time to sulk in my sorrows. I just had to survive. Going out of town required that I set a budget. The budget included rental car, plane ticket, ground transportation, hotel, food, and incidentals. I had to reconcile my budget with the company's pay to make sure I was making a profit. Every week, I made a profit. Life was good. God sent several ravens to plant seeds, but I was responsible for cultivating the ground and I was doing that quite nicely. I could look in the mirror with pride. That felt good! I couldn't point the finger at anyone else but myself. Now, I was controlling my own destiny. If I saw something in the mirror that needed to be corrected, I made the correction. During this season of my life, I learned that fires burn better when there are no ashes on the altar. I was living life and doing it with no regrets. That old mirror I once avoided finally made sense. It became useful.

"That person you see in the mirror is your reflection. It shows that even if everybody ignores you, it will always stick around with you."

Usman Ismaheel

That Old Couch

I remember when we first bought that couch. Purchasing it was a minor milestone. After losing a home and going through a period of displacement, we finally found a nice home to rent. Choosing a place was based on several factors. The school district's quality was our priority. Our children were smart; we wanted to be in a district that would provide a challenging, profitable learning experience. The new place would also have to be proximate to our places of employment. For a long period, we were driving over an hour, one-way to get to work, so we wanted to cut our commute time. Also, we wanted the new place to be close to the baseball complex where James played baseball. He was getting to the age where they practiced every day. He wasn't old enough to drive, so one of us would be tasked with taking him daily. Therefore, the new place would have to be close to the park. Another factor was the number of bedrooms. We had been cramped in two rooms much longer than we would have liked, so it was imperative that we give the children their space. We wanted each to have their own room.

While we were displaced, we stored our belongings in a local storage facility. Imagine packing a four-bedroom house into storage - in haste - and what was supposed to be a few weeks turned into three years. There were things in there we had not seen in years. Nevertheless, when we finally found a place that served our needs, we paid the first fees and moved in. It was great! A four-bedroom house in the North Cobb District with a fenced-in backyard and a sunroom. Our commutes would be shortened to less than 30 minutes. The baseball complex was a 15-minute drive and the elementary school was right around the corner. Things seemed to be turning for the better.

We took our belongings out of storage and placed them in their respective rooms. We literally had furniture for every room- beds for the bedrooms, a formal dining room set and a less formal dining set for the kitchen. We had patio furniture for the sunroom, a barbeque grill for the patio, and a nice white sofa for the living room (You know the one you let very few people sit on). We also had furniture for the den, but it was an old, sectional couch I brought from Arkansas when I first moved to Atlanta 15 years earlier. That furniture had been through the storm and the rain. It has seen several different apartments and houses, endured the rigors of three children, had been sat on, slept on, thrown up on (the baby suffered with acid reflux when she was younger, so she spit up many times on the furniture), and chosen as a place of rest for Khloe, the family dog.

The family was at a point where cleaning was no longer enough. Besides, we were in a new home with a new start. That must have been what Nikki was thinking, because one day, she asked me to find a truck to pick up furniture. We were getting a new couch, a significant seating piece in most familial settings and worthy of a closer look.

History of the Couch

The couch, also called sofa, davenport, and settee, can be traced back to ancient Egypt, where furniture was designed for reclining and built low to the floor. The couch was similar to a traditional daybed or chaise lounge. Egyptians used couches for relaxation, as well as for dining and sleeping. These early couches were wood with simplistic designs, but over time became more elaborate, often covered in luxurious materials such as leather and silk.

In ancient Greece, the couch was known as a kline, and was used for dining and relaxing. Greek couches were often made of bronze or wood and were covered in cushions and textiles. They were typically designed for one person to recline, although larger couches were also made for groups.

Throughout the Roman Empire, the couch continued to be an important part of furniture design. Roman couches, known as lectus, were often made of marble or other stone and were highly decorative. In the Middle Ages, couches were used primarily for seating and were often made of wood or stone. They were typically simple in design, with no cushions or decorative features. During the Renaissance, couches became more elaborate and were often covered in fine fabrics, such as silk and velvet. They were also often decorated with intricate carvings and ornate details. In the 18th and 19th centuries, couches continued to be an important part of furniture design. They were constructed of mahogany or other fine woods and covered in luxurious brocades and damasks. Couches were often designed to be the focal point of a room. Today's couches come in a wide variety of styles and materials, from leather and suede to synthetic fabrics and microfiber. They are an essential part of the modern living room, the designated place for relaxation, entertainment, and socializing.

My History with Couches

The couch has played an important role in my life for many years. As a young boy in Sherill, Arkansas, I entertained family and friends on the blue floral print couch in my grandmother Edna's house. Lord, if that couch could talk! Grandma Edna gave birth to 13 children and was surrounded by a plethora of grandchildren. Her house was directly opposite Antioch Missionary Baptist Church. My grandmother was an excellent cook, and her house received many visitors who sat either in the kitchen or the living room. So, that couch received its share of activity. Aside from entertaining, this couch was where we watched TV, argued with each other, sang as a family, and warmed ourselves in winter by the potbelly stove. I lived with my grandmother after my mom and dad divorced in the mid-1970s. During that time, I shared space with a few aunts and an uncle. Then Uncle C grew up and moved out, leaving me with three aunts and my grandmother. Together, we created so much culture, much of it on that couch.

Grandma Edna's couch received years of activity, but I also remember going to my great grandmother's house. We called her Granny. Granny's house was set up differently. She had both casual and formal living rooms. The couch in the living room was fair game for all kinds of activities. My little brother, uncle, and I probably wore out that couch. We watched a ton of TV, played games, wrestled, played the dozens, and did pretty much everything else on that couch. We loved that it was functional: it had a hideaway bed. We sat on it by day and slept on it at night. That was the couch in the casual living room, but she also had another couch in the formal living room, the one covered in plastic.

The plastic preserved the couch's fabric, but it was very uncomfortable. Maybe she wanted it to be uncomfortable to discourage sitting on it, except on special occasions. We didn't dare try to eat on it. The only times we sat on that couch were holidays like Easter and Christmas. We would sit in that room and open baskets and presents. That's about all it was used for. It was not good for sleeping. Have you ever tried sleeping on a couch covered in stiff plastic?

The next couch I remember was the one I grew up with living with my parents. When I say parents, I am referring to my dad and stepmom, who raised my stepsister and me. We moved from Florissant, Missouri, to North Little Rock, Arkansas, in the early 1980s. My parents decided on a 3-bedroom home with a two-car garage in a busy subdivision. This house consisted of a formal dining room and a den. The formal dining room had antique furniture, on which we rarely sat, except on special occasions. But the couch in the den was used often, especially by me. My sister loved music, so she stayed in her room quite a bit. My mom mostly stayed in her room unless she was cooking. And my dad spent his free time outside the house. Therefore, I had free access to the TV, which means I spent a great deal of time on that couch, a rust-colored sectional with tiny white polka dots. It was quite comfortable, with four sections and an ottoman. Because it was so comfortable, it got me in trouble from time to time.

Every house has rules and one parental rule was, No sleeping on the couch. When I felt myself getting sleepy, I was not supposed to fall asleep; I was supposed to go to bed. But on Saturday nights, I stayed up late to watch Saturday Night Live. The issue was that I had a hard time staying awake late. And whenever I made the mistake of lying down, it never failed. I would fall asleep. Despite the verbal warnings telling me not to, I still made the choice to lie down, thinking I could hang on. Guess what? I could not. I fell asleep almost every time. Well, choices have consequences. Mine came in the form of a stinging belt to remind me of what would happen if I decided to fall asleep, instead of going to bed.

In 1995, I made an abrupt decision to relocate to Metro Atlanta. I leased a comfortable, one-bedroom apartment in Lithia Springs. My dad made the trip from North Little Rock to bring my furniture. If memory serves me correctly, he brought my bedroom set and that sectional couch for my living room. The same couch which

I used to get whippings for falling asleep on, would now sit in my own apartment. Ironically, that same couch stayed around in some capacity for at least another 12 years. Even when Nikki and I bought our first home, that sectional went with us and took its place in the living room. We bought a nicer living room set because we had a formal living room, as well, but that sectional was a mainstay. We kicked our feet up on that couch, made love on it, changed Pampers on it (probably for all 3 children), and created culture, all on that couch. The same couch on which I got spankings proved to be a literal foundation for the family I was building.

At a certain point, we were given a new set of furniture to replace the sectional. Aesthetically, it was a more attractive set, just not as comfortable because its material was leatherette. Nevertheless, its newness enhanced the room. It was cool to sleep on (because of my history, this was necessary) if I laid my head on a pillow. But doing so without a pillow had its consequences. The only problem with that couch was that the dog liked it too much. Somewhere along the journey, we added a Yorkie we named Khloe to the family. Khloe liked to sit on the furniture, and we never tried to stop her. Khloe didn't chew shoes, but she loved chewing the fabric of that couch. It was time to move on from that set.

But there I was, needing to borrow a truck so we could go pick up the sofa Nikki found on Craigslist. We picked it up from a gentleman who was replacing that couch with a new one. You could tell that he had expensive taste, which explained why he was charging an exorbitant amount for a second-hand sofa and chair. We took them home, threw out the older furniture, and started life anew with our new furniture, at least it was new to us. Believe me, over the next several years, that furniture served us above and beyond. Kennedy was a mainstay on that couch. She constantly watched TV while doing her homework and cuddling with the dog. I could have complained, but she made straight A's. So, I didn't rock the boat. Every night, we could find her sitting on that couch with Khloe under her leg and a book or notepad in her hands, doing homework. I am certain she left a permanent, memory-foam imprint on those cushions.

Tré and McKenzie, my other two, didn't spend much time on that couch. They spent more time in their respective rooms. If memory serves correctly, by the time we got that furniture, James was in high school and extremely busy. When he was at home, he was usually in his room. The baby could be found in her room listening to music or doing her own thing. She has never been into TV. Every night at around 9 P.M., the middle child would go to bed, and I would take her place on the couch and watch TV until I fell asleep. I probably should have been upstairs creating intimacy through conversation with my spouse, but I think a part of me was trying to fall asleep on the couch so she would be asleep when I went to bed. I know. It makes no sense, but it is my truth. Familiarity breeds contempt, and a part of me was contemptuous toward the person and the relationship. So, most nights, I could be found on the couch.

Now that I think about it, I didn't just recently get stuck on the couch. Prior to this very moment, my thought was that I became stuck after my separation. But the process had begun long before the separation. Rarely did I go to bed. Instead, most nights I crawled into bed after falling asleep on that couch. Had I allowed myself to become too comfortable on the couch? How long had I been unknowingly creating this pattern? Had comfort and complacency led to these current circumstances? Maybe so. Because I was stuck like Chuck. Hindsight is always 20/20 vision; it allowed me to see things more clearly.

As badly as I wanted to get up, I couldn't. My will had been snatched and was settling deep in that sofa. Prior to separating, we lived in a rental house. So, when we decided to separate, she moved out first. When she moved, she took what she needed for their new house. Whatever she didn't want, she left. Everything else, she bought brand new. My needs are simple, so I didn't care what she took or what she left.

I remember the first night they moved out. It was official. We were legally single, now sleeping in separate homes. Nikki bought a new bed, so I kept the master and guest bedroom sets. I could have slept in the bed that I had been accustomed to sleeping in over the past 17 years, but I just could not bring myself to do it. I went to sleep right on that couch. After all, the TV was downstairs. The house sounded hollow. The TV filled the air with sound, however slight. That first night was a preview of many days to come. The silence was deafening. It yielded the semblance of noise, and I had no choice but to get used to it. Little did I know that I was turning my couch into a crutch, an enabler of sorts. I sustained injury in my personal life and had developed a limp. That couch wrapped me like a warm hug, soothing my nerves and easing my pain. It slid into position under me as its cushions became a reliable source of support.

When I moved in my apartment, I only took the bed that was in the guest bedroom and the sofa that was in the living room. I gave the master bedroom set, along with a few more items, to a young couple. I took only what I needed. I gave everything else away or sent it to the junkyard. I paid a guy to haul away everything that didn't fit in my U-HAUL. I was cool with my bed, my dining room set, and my couch.

I moved into my apartment on a Sunday. Part of the reason I chose that place is its closeness to my job. Well, when I went to work Monday, I was fired. The nerve! At least, that's how I felt. And it wasn't so much that I got fired, but it was why I got fired – for not smiling. Who smiles while going through a divorce? I must be honest. My first reaction was to plead for my job. I made the firing manager aware of how many cars I had sold so far that month. And then, it was as if Heaven opened and the Holy Spirit spoke to me directly and said, Shut up and leave. Well, I already told you this story. Anyway, I left. I drove home to my new apartment with no job and no plan. I just made one declaration. I would never give anyone the power to fire me again. So, I went home and sat on the couch for what seemed like a prolonged period.

Nights turned into days. Days seemed eternal. I sat on the couch, ate on the couch, and slept on the couch. My entire being was limited; I was not restricted to that couch. However, I chose to stay there. I had a queen-sized bed with new mattresses in the other room, but I chose to sleep on the couch. I'll be candid. I tried to sleep in the bed. I did. I would fall asleep on the couch, wake up at 3 or 4 A.M., then go get in the bed. I would probably lay there for about 30 minutes before it felt like the walls were caving in. In that darkness, I was forced to be alone with my thoughts. The TV in the living room drowned out the noises in my head. And at 4 A.M., those noises sounded louder in my bedroom. So, every night I continued the same process. I went back to the couch and would lie there until a reasonable time to wake up and go about my day of doing pretty much nothing. Besides, sleeping on the couch was a guilty pleasure; it felt as if someone was lying beside me. I felt the resistance of the back of the couch. Yes, I know that sounds crazy. I had no formal diagnosis, but I had officially lost myself. As I sit and think about it, I ask, did I lose myself? I did a little research to better understand what it means to "lose oneself."

I discovered that the phrase "losing oneself" can have different meanings depending on the context. It can refer to a state of confusion or disorientation, feeling disconnected from one's sense of identity, purpose, or values. It may also refer to a loss of one's sense of agency or control, feeling overwhelmed by circumstances, or losing touch with one's emotions.

In a psychological or spiritual sense, losing oneself can also mean experiencing a profound transformation or shift in one's consciousness or sense of self, often accompanied by a sense of unity or interconnectedness with others and the world around us. Overall, "losing oneself" can be a complex and multifaceted experience that can manifest in different ways, and the meaning can vary from person to person. It may be helpful to explore the specific context and experiences prompting the question to gain a deeper understanding of what it means for that individual. This description made sense but didn't quite resonate with me. So, I dug a little deeper.

The phrase "lose oneself" can have different meanings depending on the context in which it is used. Generally speaking, it can refer to a person feeling disconnected from their true identity or purpose, experiencing a sense of confusion or disorientation, or feeling as if they have lost the sense of self.

This feeling can arise due to various reasons, such as a major life change, a traumatic event, a mental health condition, or prolonged stress. It can manifest in different ways, such as a loss of motivation, feeling like one's life lacks direction or purpose, or a sense of detachment from one's emotions or surroundings.

In some cases, losing oneself can be a temporary experience that is resolved with time or through seeking help from a mental health professional. However, for some individuals, it can become a chronic or long-term condition that requires ongoing support to manage.

This feeling can arise due to various reasons, such as a major life change, a traumatic event, a mental health condition, or prolonged stress. It can manifest in different ways, such as a loss of motivation, feeling like one's life lacks direction or purpose, or a sense of detachment from one's emotions or surroundings.

Reflecting on the way things played out, I know now that I went through a major life change. My life was abruptly altered. It seemed as if everything was going from bad to worse. I lost a family and a job in a short span of time. I was insulted, embarrassed, angry, confused, and bereft of motivation. It was as if I lost my sense of purpose. The one thing that I had that I can honestly say that I was proud of, I lost. They were living their lives together, without me, in their own home. That messed with my mind. I felt so non-included. They were taking family portraits at holiday functions, while I was at home eating takeout from Waffle House. That messed with my head. So yes, I would say...I lost myself.

Let's revisit the story of Elijah by the Brook of Cherith:

A factor not to be overlooked in Elijah's time by the brook was its name-Cherith. The etymology of Cherith is, "the place of cutting," a place where God would perform spiritual surgery on Elijah. Here, he would supply sustenance and substance for Elijah's success. God sustained Elijah because he was willing to do what He told him to do despite how dire the circumstances. Elijah's assignment was unlike that of his counterparts. Therefore, there were only a few people with whom he could relate. I would venture to say that Elijah experienced a sense of calm at Cherith, and probably was in no hurry to leave. That is a lesson in and of itself. Please don't become too comfortable at Cherith. Zarapeth awaits.

I can relate to Elijah on so many levels. God kept me in the game based solely on the assignment He had given me, and because I was doing what he called me to do. No matter what tragedy I faced, I kept on preaching. I kept encouraging people. I kept speaking life into others' circumstances, even when I couldn't manage my own. But God would allow me to fall just so far.

Desperation is the prelude to grace.

-J. Vernon McGee

One thing we can rest our minds on is that the God who sends us somewhere is well able to keep us while we're there. For those three years, while no rain fell on the earth, water kept flowing at that brook. Not only that,

God did this during a drought. I said earlier that "Cherith" means "the place of cutting." In this case, a place where surgery was being performed to produce a new and improved Elijah. Think about it: the place of cutting. I'd like to believe that God prepared this place to perform surgery on Elijah, who had to endure what he did without anesthesia.

God didn't only see Elijah in the present, He also saw him in the future. He understood that every new level presents a new devil. So, every potential hindrance had to be removed so that Elijah would be prepared for what was to come. That is what surgery does - removes, repairs, or readjusts whatever deficiency is in the body. If all goes well, the body comes back stronger than it was in the beginning. God might not have been performing physical surgery on Elijah, but I believe He was performing spiritual surgery on him. God knew that he had a showdown with Ahab, Jezebel, and 450 false prophets on top of a mountain in a few days. God built Elijah's faith by the brook by sending ravens.

My process was similar. While I was going through, God sent several ravens-people to check on me, people who made sure I ate every day, people who got me out of the house to keep me constructively occupied. And I am extremely thankful for those people. My pastor was one of them. I didn't have to tell him what was going on, but he knew. He kept me busy helping him with weddings and funerals and aiding him daily. My church family was also a godsend during that time. I ate funeral food two or three times a day. My fridge overflowed with paper plates covered with aluminum foil and Styrofoam containers filled with leftovers. That's probably how I gained so much weight. A man can only eat so much without exercising and not expect to gain weight. But after attending the repasts, aiding my pastor with food-laden events, and stopping for takeout whenever, I came home and occupied my spot on the couch.

Pastor wasn't the only raven that showed up. I remember not having money to pay my rent. I would pay child support before paying my rent each month. I paid so much money in late fees that I could have probably paid a couple of extra months of rent. Anyway, not long after moving in my new place and losing my job, I had no idea how I was going to pay rent. That old friend who called to ask if I was working turned out to be another raven. When he told me to pack that bag and that I was going to Alabama to work at that dealership, he ushered in a modern-day miracle. At the time, I was driving my son's old 2002 Honda Accord and did not feel comfortable driving it out of town, so I let that be known.

When I look at that now, I think I was giving excuses. I was not motivated. That raven, whose name is Keith, wouldn't accept my excuses. That is, he sent that Uber and had me meet a guy who would drive me to the dealership. In a matter of moments, the ravens showed up with enough money to pay all my bills for that month. I went and worked those few days. It was only supposed to be a 3-day gig. That would have been enough to pay my bills. But God gave me more when the sale was interrupted by a snowstorm in Alabama, quite the phenomenon because it wasn't normal. I think they might have gotten 17 inches of snow. So, the sale was extended to compensate for the days missed because of the snow. I ended up working three days in that five-day span and my bills were paid for that month. When those few days were over, I went back home and took up occupancy on my couch.

Thank God that raven showed up during that season of my life. What that raven did was allow me to earn full-time wages working three days a week. I could make above-average wages working only two weekends a month. If I worked three weekends, I would have had a very good month. It was good money, but it wasn't stable. Remember I said I wasn't going to give anyone the power to fire me again? Therefore, working these contract gigs was perfect. I just could never string enough gigs back-to-back to get ahead. And when I finally did have them scheduled, the coronavirus pandemic started. I was getting a glimmer of hope only to have it eclipsed with bad news. And the ideal place for sulking was my sofa. It felt like surgery without anesthesia. My living room was the OR and my couch, the operating bed.

Thankfully, God is the surgeon.

Enough Was Enough

Have you ever felt as if you were living on Barely Get Along Boulevard or Had Enough Avenue? If so, how did you respond? Did you view it as a temporary place? Or did you install a mailbox? If you did the latter, you might have prolonged your moment. Neither of those addresses was meant to be permanent. They were meant to be temporary.

Elijah was never supposed to stay by the brook. Little did he know that his time there would be limited, and he did not need to get comfortable. Zarapeth was his next destination. I had to think about that. Was Elijah going through a process or was he on a journey? They sound similar, but are very different. In general, a process refers to a series of steps or actions taken to achieve a particular goal or outcome. A journey usually refers to a long trip or experience one goes through to reach a destination or achieve a personal goal. God was using Elijah's life to achieve an outcome that would shock the world and cause men to know Him. Conversely, while sitting on the couch, I was reminded that although I was on a personal journey, it was part of a process. Zarapeth was just a pit stop.

In its etymology, Zarapeth means "the place of refining." It is where one goes to recover following surgery. There, nurses begin the process of nurturing the body back to a place of self-sufficiency. Administering anesthesia will give the body a chance to wean itself from medications. Applying oxygen will allow the person to begin breathing on their own. Various attendants do what is necessary to move the body toward complete healing. During that time, they limit visitation to ward off the individual's exposure to infection. That was a good time for Elijah to spend intimate time with God; he was able to reflect on his experiences. God had used him mightily, so he had experienced life's highs. But, now that he was on the run, he might have initially looked at this as one of the lows. Even in this low place, God met all his needs. So, why focus on the negatives? Elijah needed a positive mindset.

Dwayne Woods composed a song with these lyrics:

As soon as I stopped worrying

Worrying how the story ends

That's when I let go and let God

Let God have His way.

That's when things started happening

When I stopped looking back

I let go and let God have his way.

That is indeed my testimony. While sitting on that couch, I experienced an epiphany, that sudden, profound insight that leads to a new understanding of a situation, problem, or idea. Often described as a moment of acute clarity, an epiphany brings a new level of awareness. An epiphany can be triggered by a variety of experiences, such as a sudden realization after a period of contemplation, a conversation that offers a fresh perspective, or a life-changing event that causes a shift in thinking. The experience is often described as a feeling of enlightenment or a sudden "aha!" moment.

An epiphany can have a significant impact on an individual's life, leading to changes in behavior, beliefs, and attitudes. It can inspire creative breakthroughs, prompt personal growth and development, and offer new solutions to previously intractable problems. My epiphany came after a series of experiences, and those experiences led me back to Someone bigger than I, Someone with the power to change my circumstances for the better.

I felt like the younger son in the Prodigal Son narrative in Luke 15. In this familiar story, a young man went to his father and asked for his inheritance while he was still alive, which was within his rights. The father obliged. The Bible says that afterwards, the young man went to a far country and "wasted his substance on riotous living." In other words, he lived a reckless lifestyle and ended up broke. Eventually, he got a job tending to hogs, which was against his culture. He knew that he had reached rock bottom when while feeding them, he found himself considering eating what the hogs were eating. That's deep. I spoke about spending time at my grandmothers' homes. One of them, the late Edna Kirklin, raised hogs. I knew we would slaughter at least one annually for food, but I'm not sure what she did with the rest of them.

My chores included burning the trash and feeding the hogs. I vividly remember two barrels, one for trash and one for slop. Slop was what the hogs ate. Slop consisted of all the leftovers we didn't eat, including bones. We didn't have a garbage disposal, so we threw all our leftovers in that barrel. It was exposed to the elements, so it would get rained in, causing it to become soupy. I would scoop the slop out of the barrel with a bucket and pour it in the hogs' trough so they could eat. It was disgusting. I couldn't imagine myself eating what they were eating, but thankfully, I have never been that hungry. But that was part of the Prodigal's plight. Everyone has to go through a process before being promoted. Unfortunately, until we experience that epiphany, we might inadvertently prolong the process. We will find ourselves circling the same mountain or going through the same issue for an extended period when we should have learned our lesson and moved on.

I could relate to that young man in so many ways. Many times I felt as if I was in a foreign place. I found myself doing things I was not accustomed to doing. The culture I helped create was going on without me, but I had to continue life in my current circumstances. I was not adjusting as quickly as I thought I would. I had spent all my humanistic know-how and ingenuity, but I couldn't manipulate my way out of this one. I needed divine help. I needed God to remind me who I was. That young man came to himself in a pig pen. I came to myself on my couch in the living room of my apartment. I was tired of the way I was living. I was right there with Fannie Lou Hamer declaring, I'm sick and tired of being sick and tired. Finally, enough was enough.

What was enough and how is it quantified in time? How long? One year? Two years? 10 years? 20 years? I mean, really? How long is long enough? Of course, that is a rhetorical question; there is no one-size-fits-all answer. If that question were posed to a large group of people, the answers would vary. Some would answer quickly because they are fast learners. Others might not learn as fast, so it might take longer. It doesn't matter how long it takes. What matters most is that the scales of guilt fall from our eyes and that we can see clearly, gaining a better view of our purpose. For a season, I thought God had fired me. I wasn't considering eating what the hogs were eating, but I was probably associating with some of their behavior patterns, and I was quite familiar with the way hogs live.

Taking care of the hogs involved supplying them water. Summers in Sherrill, Arkansas, in the late 1970s and early 80s, were extremely hot. When no rain fell, the ground became very dry. The hogs still needed water. I would take a water hose to supply water for the hogs. I would spray water all over their pen, on them, on the dirt, and in their trough. The hogs loved it. Eventually the water began to mix with the dirt and form mud. As humans, we try to avoid mud because we know the limitations that it offers. It's slippery. One can become stuck in it. And if he's not careful, he might find himself wallowing in it.

In Psalm 40, the psalmist implies that he had been stuck in a horrible pit, which had a floor consisting of miry clay. That's mud. No human should feel comfortable wallowing in mud. That's what hogs do. They are comfortable in the mud. What's comfortable to one person, might stand for being stuck to another. When a person is comfortable wallowing in mud, going through the same things over and over and never learning from them, that's equivalent to hoggish behavior.

You think I would have learned after the first repossession or after the first foreclosure. Surely, I would have learned my lesson after being caught in and forgiven for the affair. Nikki forgave me. She said, "James, I wipe your slate clean." That should have been enough. By not learning from my mistake and changing my behavior, was I wallowing in the mud? The Prodigal had gone through a lot, but he was determined not to let the muddy hog pen, where slop was the only thing on the menu, represent his final chapter. He was raised in a structured environment that provided his every need, but here he was, associating with hogs, wanting. He was hungry.

Again, I can relate. When I think about what I was used to versus how I was living, I went through a plethora of emotions. First of all, I was angry. I was upset because of all the things I sacrificed by not properly managing my blessings. One of my favorite New Testament writers is the Apostle Paul. In Philippians 3:8, he tells of how he counted all things as "loss" in exchange for getting an opportunity to know Jesus. In the Greek, the word loss means *forfeit*. Paul was saying that he willingly gave up those things, because God was more important. And there is a difference between something being counted as loss and outright losing something. With loss, one gives up things willingly. If one lost something, he didn't do it willingly. He mismanaged or mishandled it, so he lost it. Sitting there on that couch, those were my thoughts. This was my epiphany, my defining moment. For a long time, because my shoulders are broader, I bore the entire burden of responsibility for my current lot in life. I said everything was my fault. Nothing about what I was going through felt normal.

That was one of my emotions, but I also felt thankful that I survived. I didn't die on the journey. I didn't give up. I didn't throw in the towel. I had every reason to quit, but I couldn't. The Scripture verse begins, "Now unto Him who is able to keep us from falling..." The key word is *keep*. In this context, the word keep means to preserve. The word preserve presents the idea of something being kept from spoiling. Circumstances certainly tried to spoil me, but they were unsuccessful. What kinds of circumstances? I'm glad you asked.

- I faced evictions several times.

- I went without cable television. I understand cable is a luxury. But I had not gone without it since living in my parent's home. I watched local channels with an antenna. I did have Wi-Fi, so I was able watch some shows on my firestick. But the antenna was sufficient.

- I remember Scana Natural Gas cutting off the gas because I forgot to pay the past due amount on the bill. That meant I had to pay the whole bill, current and past due. I didn't have the money. To make matters worse, that meant that I couldn't light the pilot light on my hot water heater. This was during the cold months when hot water and heat were necessary. BUT... mine was cut off! Faced with this reality, I had to adjust. The gas was off, but the electricity was still on. So, I went out and bought an electric heater to keep the rooms warm. I was able to move it from room to room. I like sleeping in the cold under the covers, anyway. That took care of the heating issue. As far as hot water was concerned, that was easy. I had an electric stove. I just boiled water in pots for bathwater. I think I boiled 10 large pots of water per day. It was tedious, but effective.

In 1990, I was a first-year student at the University of Arkansas-Pine Bluff. On the first day of class, Professor David Dedrick asked us what made us human beings.

Many students tried to answer, but all were wrong. Finally, after hearing all our wrong answers, he gave us his answer. What was his answer? He said that our ability to adapt is what makes us human beings. No matter what position we find ourselves in, we can survive because of our ability to adapt.

Dedrick cautioned, however, that while we are adapting, we must not make the mistake of acquiescing. The difference between these two can mean achieving a goal or making an excuse for not achieving it. While the mindset of acquiescence is "Whatever," the mindset of adaptation is "I got this!" To acquiesce is to give in, to fold, to go along to get along. Acquiescing is passive and easy. I know; I became quite adept at it, attending church events because it was my duty, or showing up at birthday celebrations out of a sense of obligation, not motivation. At home and at work, I found myself doing things halfheartedly, generally accepting change with neither challenge nor argument.

Conversely, to adapt is to adjust to change. In fact, much of our daily contentment depends on how we adapt to the ongoing changes in our lives. When circumstances change or when disruptions occur or when – Heaven forbid - one partner leaves the partnership, we are left to adjust to a new reality or be stuck in some interminable state of nonproductivity. I did not want a divorce, but Nikki did, and in the final analysis, her decision to part ways became my new reality. It was on me to adapt. I tried to keep my sadness private, but I'm certain people could tell at times that I was not myself. I was no longer "married man living with wife, children, job, house and dog." Rev. James H. Kirklin was "single man living alone with apartment and job."

Bishop C. L. Oliver often used the illustrations of "saturating in sorrow" and "marinating in misery." For far too long, that is exactly what I had been doing: feeling sorry for myself, trapped in an endless loop, choosing despair, associating with hoggish behaviors. I acquiesced to general lethargy. My routine was: Wake up and watch TV. Find something outside to do. Distract myself with aimless pursuits. Wake up again and watch more TV. This was my routine, and I was perfectly fine with it. I had schoolwork to keep me busy. I was still trying to complete an M.Div., which might sound crazy, but I could not allow my evolving marital drama to interfere with preparation for ministry. My days were the definition of insanity: repeating the same behavior over and over and expecting a different result. Eventually, I stopped looking for a different result. Like the Prodigal son, I got comfortable in the mud.

Dr. Donald L. Parsons of Chicago's Logos Baptist Assembly, advised, "When you find yourself in a valley, you employ valley tactics, one of which is connecting dots." I became a spiritual detective in the valley, collecting dots. But it was not until I connected those dots – *positive attitude* plus *positive actions* equal *positive results* – that I was able to crawl out of that valley. In retrospect, acquiescing brought pain and defeat; adapting brought reconciliation and peace. I am thankful that I survived, but disappointed that I put myself in that position. I should have noticed the signs. Enough was enough.

I Needed to Sit Down

I had the pleasure of spending many of my formative years at my grandmothers' homes in a little Arkansas community called Sherrill-Pastoria. I grouped the communities because they are directly next to each other, and I divided my time between the two grandmothers. I had similar experiences at both of their homes. I remember certain things, specifically. For instance, I remember all the open land around their houses. I also remember all the fruit trees around their houses: plums, apples, pears; if I'm not mistaken, one grandmother even grew peaches. In fact, I know that to be true, because she made peach preserves.

I have very personal memories of my grandmothers. I remember walking down beside the fields and picking blackberries with Grandmother Edna. She smelled like baby powder, all the time. She would start cooking dinner for my aunts and uncles not long after serving breakfast. And this was a daily routine. It was nothing for me to be awakened to the smell of bacon, eggs, oatmeal, and butter biscuits. Of course, I had chores. I had to burn the trash. In the country, we didn't have the luxury of a garbage disposal, so I had to slop the hogs; they were the country garbage disposal. When picking season came, I watched my aunts and uncles go into the fields to pick peas and cotton. That's how they made money for school clothes. Some of these poignant memories have stayed with me.

One memory I will never forget is the sky's transformation when storms were in that area. Remember, this was the country. It was quite rural and consisted of wide, open spaces. So, if a storm was coming, you could see it from miles away. The sky would divide into light and darkness, as if two armies were meeting in the middle of the air preparing to collide, but the light always gave way to the darkness when it came to storms. And old folk were different. They respected storms.

As soon as a storm started to brew, both my grandmas would tell us to sit down somewhere and let the Lord do his work. That was so powerful to me. Granny Jamie Lee Mazique would sit in her chair and just start rocking. As she rocked, she prayed. You would have felt the spirit enter the room. Granny would fall into a trance while talking to the Lord. I was young, but for some reason, I understood spiritual things. My little brother would ask me what was wrong with Granny, and I would have to tell him, nothing. Granny is just praying. And her prayers were different when she prayed during the storms. She would pray until heaven got the news. She used the pressure from the storm to take her prayers higher. That's what eagles do. They use the pressure from the storm to take them higher. Put a pin right there.

I came to discover that I would never have tapped into my power again had I not sat down. Interestingly enough, God made me sit down. In Luke 9:13-17, Jesus feeds 5,000 men, besides women and children. I noted that John was the only gospel writer who noticed that

Jesus specifically told the disciples to seat the men first. Jesus had reasons for doing that. First, he wanted the men in the crowd to be counted. Notice, John numbered the men, but not the women and children. Men were the leaders of their families, the heads of their households. He knew that if the men sat down, the women and children would follow. They lived in a different day and age. In their society, women followed the men, and, in most cases, the men were worthy to be followed. So, when the men sat down, the women and children sat down, too. The other reason he had the men sit down was to show them as calm in a crisis. If the family saw the men as calm in what was typically chaotic, then the rest would learn how to respond during adversity.

"Sitting down" had similar ramifications for me. Sitting down reminded me that I still mattered. I still counted and others were counting on me. My children, my family and friends, were counting on me. More than anything, sitting on the couch allowed me to remain calm. Shut-off notices lay on the table, but the lights never got cut off due to non-payment. The cell phone company got its money every month. They repossessed the car one time, but I got it back the same day. I endured my share of storms and some of them were devastating. My consolation lay in knowing that Jesus works the night shift. Some of the things I went through were undeniably dark. But if he works the night shift, I might as well go to sleep at night. Why stay up during a storm knowing he had everything under control? He controls storms and he can stop storms. At least, that was what I had been preaching and teaching for over 25 years. I just needed to be reminded. When I came to this discovery, I got off the couch and got back in the bed. It was time for proper rest.

As I said earlier, in life, we pick up habits, some of them wicked, and those habits become lifestyles. Over the years, we fall into routines and those routines become our "normals." When our circumstances change, we develop new normals. I was not accustomed to sleeping alone. When Nikki and I were married, even when we went to bed angry, we still slept in the same bed. Lying in bed with someone allows you to feel the warmth of a body. And because one of my love languages is touch, just the fact that someone is there supplies a sense of peace. Well, no one else was in my bed. I was alone, all by myself and I did not feel peace. In fact, I felt the opposite - desolate, dark, and dismal. I could not sleep in that bed. So, I started sleeping on the couch. Before I knew it, I could sleep only on the couch. That was my new normal.

It took a while, but I finally figured out the reason. I said this earlier but sleeping on the couch offered just enough resistance, as if someone was lying beside me. I know it sounds strange, but it is what it is. That was the only place I could sleep in my apartment- on my couch. I found that odd because I could sleep in other beds. If I visited my parents' home, I could sleep there. In a hotel or Airbnb, I had no problem sleeping. I just could not sleep in that bed. But I could sleep like a baby on the couch. So, I wasn't just sitting on it, I was also sleeping on it, and in fact, spending most of my time on the couch. I was stuck.

Spending all that time on the couch allowed me to do a lot of thinking and reflecting. Eventually, those thoughts turned into dreams and those dreams evolved into reminders, reminders of what God had already promised me. I still believe that His promises are still Yea and Amen. If He allows you to see it, it is custom made for you. You must seize it. Sitting on the couch of "do nothing, doing nothing" will yield those results- NOTHING. My doing nothing changed nothing about His promise and plan for my life. I just had to do my part. These were the thoughts that flooded my mind as I sat there reflecting and enjoying God's reminders. Sitting on the couch was therapeutic. I didn't realize it at first, but time later revealed otherwise. I *needed* to sit down.

So, here is the question: When does one need to sit down? One needs to sit down when he is running with no real destination in mind. And it's fine to run if the run is calculated. But if one is running but isn't going anywhere, he might need to sit down. I was running with no real sense of direction. I would get great ideas, take off running, lose momentum, and not follow through with those ideas. As I have matured. I have learned that momentum must be properly channeled. A river consists of many streams and tributaries that all flow into the same river. If the water flow isn't clearly directed, certain sections of the river can become overwhelmed, potentially causing floods.

This reminds me of my first high school track meet. We were running the Mills Relays at Little Rock Mills High

School. Coach Bowers entered me in the 400-meter dash. Let me say this: I didn't even want to run track. He made me run track. Anyway, Coach put me in the 400-meter dash because he said I had a long stride. Mind you, I never actually ran a 400-meter dash. In practice, I worked out with the sprinters, and we would usually work out in parameters of 300 meters. Sets of 100s, 200s, and 300s. At my best, I could probably run 300 meters in 34 seconds. So, I figured I could run the last 100 in 15 seconds and be OK. Wrong! At 300 meters, that monkey jumped on my back, and everyone passed me. It was down to me and one other guy. I wanted to quit because I was taking part in a race I was losing, so why should I finish? No one remembers the loser. At least, those were my thoughts. But I heard my father's voice, yelling from the sideline, telling me to run faster. Almost everyone had finished the actual race. But another race developed within the actual race, a race between me and the last guy. We were down to the last 25 or 30 meters, both neck and neck, trying to cross the finish line first. Both of us seemed to gain a burst of energy, giving us a will to win THIS race. The good news is that I won. You know how I won? I finished. Why run if you're not going to finish? That was one of my problems. That was one of the complaints in my marriage. I started stuff but didn't finish. That's why finishing a degree at the age of 38 was so gratifying. I finished something that I started.

It wasn't that I didn't want to finish. In my mind, I did finish. My mind processes differently. I see a thing in its beginning and ending. I don't always see the process.

Subconsciously my mind thinks that it has done its job by coming up with the idea. And that's the thing. An idea is just that- an idea.

I Do Everything Alone.

The challenge is to promote an idea to a vision. Because I didn't do that, my mind went on to other ideas. I believe a Sower scatters seed and I considered myself a Sower. Seed is useless if it stays on the surface and is not planted. I would put ideas out, give them to people, and hope they would run with them. That was my mistake. The prophet, Habakkuk, said to write the vision, but he also said to make it plain. I was giving the vision but not making it plain. Therefore, people couldn't run with the vision I was presenting. I could see how people thought I was running but going nowhere. Maybe that's why God sat me down.

Or maybe He sat me down because of things I had done in the past that people helped me cover up, instead of sitting me down. Maybe I should have been sat down when I made my first mistake. I flirted with Hell and got burned. I was going places where I shouldn't have been, availing myself of temptations I knew were detrimental to my ministry. An old hymn we sing in church asks, How can I live in sin and feel the Savior's love? I was doing some questionable things and going to church on Sunday, preaching as if I had done nothing wrong.

Honestly, I wish I could have been at church every day. It was safer and I loved nothing more than preaching.

To be candid, I used to hate the time after I preached because it was such a letdown because I didn't know when I would experience that feeling again. When I came down from that emotional and spiritual high, I had to channel that energy somewhere, and I usually channeled it into the wrong places. I tried to hide but as you know, you can only cover things up so long and God will only allow you to get away with certain things until He gets tired. Then you have a choice. You either keep going and get exposed or you sit down and get it right. Sometimes we make the choice and sometimes He makes the choice for us. Fortunately *and* unfortunately, He made the choice for me. That's why I needed to sit down.

God wanted to humble me, and I didn't get it, at first. Clearly there were times that I kept going when I should have stepped back. I remember back in the late 1990s, I was leaving work headed somewhere I had no business going, driving a 1991 Honda Civic. I drove from Willett Honda in Morrow, GA, riding on Jonesboro Rd. One of my coworkers was following me. I remember looking in the rearview mirror to see if he was behind me, making the turn I was making. Before I knew it, Bam! I had a head on collision. Everything seemed to stop. I was driving at least 45 mph but that didn't matter. The impact of that SUV knocked me backwards. I remember sitting there in shock, not believing what had just happened to me. I literally had a head on collision. I could have died. I think the seatbelt helped save me because I didn't move. I have worn a seatbelt since one saved my dad's life when I was little boy. I remember my mom's face when she received the phone call telling her what happened. Thankfully, I was okay. Everything was intact. I could still move my legs. I had the activity of all my faculties. I was coherent, so that means I wasn't knocked out and was not dead. My ego was a little bruised because I knew my car was totaled, but I was okay. I called Nikki and told her what happened, jumped in the car with my friend, and went home. An ambulance came and the medic asked if I needed a ride to the hospital, but I said no. I went home and in fact, went to church the next day. I was a little sore and my body ached, but I went on with business as usual.

I should have sat down and reflected on what just happened. Many people do not walk away from what I had survived. That probably was a good place to humble myself and change the course of my life. Good thing our hopes and dreams don't come with expiration dates. Instead, they re-present themselves when we are sufficiently mature to receive what hope is offering. Now that I was sitting down, I was able to focus on projects I had not finished over the years, This time it was easier because it was as if I had done it before. Everything I needed done, I had done aspects of before or had some knowledge of. That made things a little easier. Sitting down helped.

At one point in my life, I didn't have a problem focusing. I recall an incident from the Spring and Fall of 1994. I was an In School Suspension (ISS) teacher in the North Little Rock School District. When high school students were suspended, they were required to report to my class to complete their suspensions. During that week, I assigned them to write a 10-page paper listing their infractions. Other than that, they had to do their homework. When they finished their homework, they had to be quiet. All that quietness allowed me to focus, so I did a lot of reading. I had an insatiable desire to learn. I accepted my call to ministry in January of that same year and wanted to know what I was talking about when I preached. So, I read.

During that time, I was working with a talent similar to a photographic memory. Retention was easier because I was able to focus. Here is the problem. I only focused when I felt I needed to focus. I wasn't focused all the time. Listen, just because I was able to focus didn't mean that I had discipline. A person can focus when it is convenient for them and not be disciplined. If they are truly disciplined, their focus won't waver. It will remain consistent. Truthfully, I was the world's worst procrastinator. I focused on what interested me and the things that were necessary. When I refer to "necessary" things, I am referring to things like writing a sermon or completing schoolwork. When I needed to, I was able to turn my focus on and really lock in to finish projects on a case-by-case basis. If it was necessary or interesting, I stayed focused until I completed the project. Perhaps, that is why I was able to finish an undergraduate degree while working a full-time job, with a family, while being borderline homeless and was able to do so *magna cum laude*. My undergraduate degree was more difficult to obtain than the graduate degree because I had to attend class. With the graduate degree(s), work was easier because all I had to do was focus on the syllabus and rubric. They laid out expectations for the class. If I met the required expectation, at the very least, I would pass the class. I did more than pass. I always kept an A average because I was able to focus. I remember writing 10-page papers on the last day and getting A's. But notice what I said, I had to turn it on. Until I turned it on, it was off.

So, it wasn't that I lacked focus; I just didn't execute. I had an on/off switch, which remained in the off position. I don't know what it was. Perhaps I didn't want to operate with the discipline necessary to attain and sustain success. I don't know. Or maybe unbeknown to me, I was afraid of failure. If I didn't start, I couldn't fail. The problem is that type of mentality can leave a person in a state of stagnation. A lot of things came easily for me early in life. School was always easy. I made good grades without having to study much. I wrote papers at the last minute, crammed for exams, and never failed tests. I was able to comprehend most things quickly. I thought I was on the right trajectory because life was easy.

I moved to Atlanta in 1995 and started selling cars at a dealership in Duluth, Georgia. I bounced around from dealership to dealership before I finally settled down and advanced into management at only 26 years old. Upward mobility came with its share of perks, including a sizable monthly salary guarantee. It was the wrong mentality to have, but my thoughts were that I made that amount of money before we sold our first car. I was making a guaranteed six figures, but I was looking at the door, hoping a $40K a year church would rescue me. The truth is, I was just never passionate about the car business. I loved the immediate gratification that it provided, and it probably could have made me rich. But I had other aspirations. If I had my way, I would have been traveling across the country preaching in a different city each night. That's why I was never as successful in the car business as I could have been. I didn't take it seriously enough.

The potential was limitless, but I had to work long hours, weekends, and holidays. I missed so much family time working. My son James played high-level baseball and had to travel to out-of-town tournaments. One team he played with was the East Cobb Astros. One Fall, they traveled to away-games every weekend. Whether it was Charleston, SC or Jupiter, FL, they were playing baseball somewhere. Guess where I was? At work. The sad part is that even though I was at work, I was not focused on selling cars. I was online checking scores and more importantly, I wanted to see how my son was doing in the games. I felt it every time he struck out. I rejoiced every time he got a hit. Just imagine how I reacted when he hit a home run...ecstatic! Imagine how much I focused on sales while I was supposed to be selling. In fact, I started to build some level of resentment towards the business. I lost my will to sell cars, but I still had a desire to make money. I started and stopped several businesses. I dibbled and dabbled in the mortgage business. I ran a shoeshine stand in an office building in Buckhead, an upscale community in Atlanta. I was in the company of business moguls, lawyers, and financiers. My clients were pastors who drove to Buckhead to drop off their shoes. I saw several celebrities, including T.I. and T-Boz, and even gave T.I. a couple of my Project R.O.B. T-shirts. I believe God placed me there so that I would come into the company of great men. I should have sat down and taken advantage of those opportunities, but I didn't, and perhaps now, God was ordering me to sit down.

The truth is, I was tired. My Midas touch had turned into a mud touch. Things that used to work, worked no longer. I had exhausted my humanistic know-how and ingenuity. I had reached my existential breaking point, experiencing prophetic burnout, much like the Prophet Elijah did when he sat under the juniper tree in I Kings 19. He asked the Lord to take his life when Jezebel put a bounty on his head for killing the 450 false prophets of Baal. This pronouncement frightened Elijah, which was strange, considering how God consistently used Him to accomplish miracles. He was sustained at the Brook of Cherith during a drought in I Kings 17:4-6. A woman chose to feed him first instead of feeding herself and found that her meal barrel never emptied, and the jar of oil never ran out (I Kings 17:8-16). He had already revived the widow's son (I Kings 17:17-24). My point is that Elijah had personally seen the hand of God at work in his life. Yet, there he was sitting under a very specific tree with suicidal thoughts. Juniper trees produce a fruit that functions as a male contraceptive. Contraceptives prevent female eggs from being fertilized by male sperm. Elijah sat there; he could do nothing for God. How could he perform miracles if he was stuck under a tree? Elijah had been made ineffective and unproductive.

As with the Prodigal son, I can relate to Elijah. I, too, have seen the hand of God move in my life...on several occasions. I have lain hands on the sick and watched them recover. I witnessed Him deliver me from two car accidents. He saved my father from heart attacks in 1994 and 2023, prolonging his life. I have seen God make ways out of no ways on Christmases when we were lacking. Someway and somehow, the children always found something under the tree, and the travel baseball and softball fees always got paid. Amid chaos and confusion, God proved Himself time and time again. These provisions might seem insignificant to others, but they were signs for me that He was indeed Jehovah-Jireh, God Who provides. He was just as much God with me when I was stuck on the couch, as He was when I was in a sanctuary laying hands on the sick. If He was using me to do things in the life of others, why was I sitting here stuck on the couch? Maybe He made me sit down because I needed to be sat down.

Coaches sit players down when they are not performing to their full potential. Every team has a starting lineup that consists of individuals who work best together to carry out what the coach wants accomplished. If one of the starters is lacking in his responsibilities, there is always a substitute willing to come in and take the starter's place. That is why the starters must constantly work to keep their jobs. They must know the playbook, the tendencies of their opponent, and the coach's expectations. My playbook was and is the Bible, and I recognize the enemy's characteristics. God is the coach and His expectations for the game are written in the playbook. My job is to execute the plays. I had not been executing, so I had been sat down.

I remember in my senior year of high school, I played on a basketball team at the Boys Club where my dad was the coach. We had a good team. Most of the players on our team played for the school in junior high, but never grew any taller and were better at football. We won most of the games we played. However, during one game that I remember, I was acting moody and being overly sensitive. Our players were criticizing me, and I just wasn't having it. One of my pet peeves is being embarrassed in public and my teammates knew this. We happened to be playing our main rivals, who also happened to have a very good team. We were just better. Well, at half time, I went down to the other end of the court and told the other team how to beat us. I know. That was vindictive. My dad, who was our coach, threatened to whip me because of my behavior. Anyway, they adhered to my strategy and executed perfectly.

The lead we had at half-time dwindled. Over the course of the next few minutes, I calmed down. Sitting on the bench gave me a different perspective and allowed me to review my actions. I realized that I had messed up. Thankfully, I got a chance to redeem myself. With only a couple of minutes left in the fourth quarter, I hit three key free throws to help solidify the win. Sitting changed my perspective and presented a different view of my situation, as chaotic as it seemed. Maybe that is why I needed to sit down, to gain a different perspective on all that had gone wrong in my life.

I have heard different expressions with regards to individuals who go to prison. Of course, we have heard it said that they were sentenced to prison or jail. But I have also heard it referred to as "going on vacation," "going up the road," or "doing time."

Another expression I believe is applicable is that the person is going "to sit down" for a certain period. During the time that they are "sitting down," they can reflect on their mistakes and develop life skills to function outside of a life of crime. At least, that is what should happen. It used to happen more frequently, before prisons became profit centers for corporations. In the late 80s and early 90s, prisons became privatized. Companies that own prisons trade publicly on the NYSE. You know as well as I do that companies on the exchange only want to increase their bottom line. Therefore, they will cut costs by any means necessary, no matter who the casualties are. That is part of the reason the recidivism rate is so high, because very little rehabilitation takes place. So, the person who has been incarcerated must take responsibility for why he/she is sitting down. They must face certain realities:

#1) They are 100% responsible for their own choices and those choices carry consequences; and

#2) They alone can change the course or direction, if they take advantage of available resources.

Yesterday is a canceled check and tomorrow is a promissory note. All we have is today, and we must learn to take full advantage of it. These are some of the lessons I learned while I was sitting down. I needed to sit down.

#OnThePathToBetter

Don't sit down and wait for opportunities to come.

Get up and make them.

-Madam C. J. Walker

No person was better equipped to utter these words than Madam C. J. Walker, an African American entrepreneur, philanthropist, and social justice advocate. The *Guinness Book of World Records* lists her as the first female, self-made millionaire in America. Notice what I said: Madam C. J. Walker was self-made. She could have used valid rationales embraced by many during those days: slavery, poverty, hunger, and beatings, among them. Think about it. Walker was born in 1867, not long after the Emancipation Proclamation freed enslaved African Americans. That was a difficult period for Black people, even though they represented most of the skilled laborers in the country. Despite the racial challenges of the time, Walker became an entrepreneur and achieved something that had nothing to do with agriculture. She made a fortune by developing and marketing a line of cosmetics and hair care products for Black women. Had she accepted her assigned role as a second-class citizen, she would have missed out on all that was available for her. She overcame two strikes imposed against her: 1) she was female, and 2) she was Black.

Nevertheless, Madam Walker rose above these alleged so-called negative attributes and became a millionaire in the 1900s, quite an accomplishment. It demonstrates that if a person sets their mind to something, they can carry it out. So, to hear her message about seizing the moment hits a bit differently, considering how she advanced despite adversities. True enough, I faced my share of adversities. Lord knows I did. Some were self-inflicted and I believe some were God-inflicted. The self-inflicted wounds hurt more and lasted a lot longer.

As I emphasized earlier, choices have consequences. Try coupling consequences with a conscience. That's tough, and it can cause you to stay in adverse situations longer than necessary. I allowed my life to be placed on pause. That was 100% on me and I accept the responsibility. It was my fault. I knew better. I had all that insurance and did not make a claim when I needed to. The Apostle Paul said it: Let the same mind be in you that was also in Christ Jesus (Philippians 2:5). I should have listened.

God-inflicted adversities are different. God has a purpose in allowing us to go through whatever we find ourselves going through. Do you remember Job? Job 1:1 describes Job as a man who feared God and eschewed (shunned) evil. In the eyes of man and God, he was one who walked with integrity. Everyone should wish to walk in wholeness. Integrity is not what you show outwardly; it is how you behave when no one is watching. Job was that guy, but God still offered him up to be tempted by Satan. God had a plan for Job.

*6Now there was a day when the sons
of God came to present themselves
before the LORD, and Satan came
also among them. 7And the LORD
said unto Satan, Whence comest
thou? Then Satan answered the
LORD, and said, From going to and
fro in the earth, and from walking up
and down in it. 8And the LORD said
unto Satan, Hast thou considered my
servant Job, that there is none like
him in the earth, a perfect and an
upright man, one that feareth God,
and escheweth evil?*

Notice a couple of things in this text:

1. Satan came to the meeting when the "sons of God" came to present themselves before God. Did Satan feel he had to present himself as well?

2. When Satan was seeking someone to devour (I Peter 5:8), God suggests Job. Why would He suggest Job if He didn't feel Job could be trusted?

Considering that God is omniscient and knows the end at the beginning, He knew the outcome before Satan attacked Job. Satan did what was his purpose to do: kill, steal, and destroy Job. But Job resolved that, though slain, he would continue to trust in the Lord (Job 13:15). He said in all his appointed time, he would wait until his change came (14:14b). That is the proper mindset and the one that I discovered worked best for me. No matter what happened, I was going to trust in the Lord. That would be the only way I could get off the couch...and on the path to better.

Act like you got it before you get it.

Job's story illustrates principles that will aid individuals who are stuck on the couch and desire to get off. These principles fuel church colloquialism, to which I am relentlessly accustomed. One such principle is that you should, "Act like you got it before you get it." The first time I heard this was at Atlanta's Mt. Nebo Baptist Church, from one of its associate ministers. What a declaration of faith! This is a powerful statement because it suggests that you don't have to wait until the battle is over, you can do a premeditated shout. You can dance in advance, even while smack dab in the middle of it, whatever your "it" may be. Acting like you have it before you physically have it, is like calling the unseen as seen (Romans 4:17). It is like being in a storm, expecting the sunshine, and watching dark clouds roll away. But prior to their rolling away, you called it. You *knew* that brighter days were coming, so you expressed it, and it came to pass. The ability to call the unseen as seen requires healthy cognitive skills.

Cognitive skills, or intellectual skills, are mental processes that enable us to receive, process, understand, and use information. These skills play a crucial role in how we think, learn, problem-solve, and interact with the world around us. Cognitive skills encompass a range of abilities. They can be grouped into various categories, all of which help when it comes to seeing ourselves in situations better than the ones we are currently in. Those groups include memory, attention, problem-solving, decision-making, feeling, and information processing. When we are using these abilities at their most, we can usually look beyond our bleak circumstances and see winning instead of losing. Job was a good example.

Job was sick! He was sitting in sackcloth and ashes, scraping his boils, trying to get relief from an unrelentless pain. His wife made the ridiculous suggestion that he should curse God and die. Imagine that. The soulmate who is supposed to be his confidant is shattering his confidence. She knew his routine. She probably made him fresh chicory every morning before he went out to make daily sacrifices. When he came home, she undoubtedly had a good traditional breakfast waiting on the table. Mrs. Job saw the hand of God move in Job's life many times. It had to be hard to see her man suffering, to witness his going through conditions he could not control. She wanted to see him relieved of misery, so she uttered those unthinkable words, "Curse God and die." Imperatively and irresponsibly, she made this erroneous suggestion, considering nothing else worked. She thought God would certainly have rescued Job, since Job had kept his integrity throughout the years. But no emancipator came. He had to endure sickness and suffering. In the face of a wife whose faith was failing and friends whose suggestions were stressful, Job made the conscious decision to trust God and wait. Wait.

Traditionally, we have understood the word "wait" to mean, stay where you are, or delay action until another time, or until something else happens. The word comes from a Hebrew phrase which means "to tarry" or "to wait with expectancy." One waits with expectancy when one expects the situation to change. That's why Job could make this bold statement. Things might not be going my way now and in fact, may never go my way again. But even if circumstances don't change, with the little time I have left, I am going to wait on my change to come. I felt Job on that one. For the past few years, things have not necessarily gone my way. I have lost a lot. But the one thing I did not lose was my love for and trust in God. There were times that I did not feel loved, but feelings are not factual. God was there the entire time...being God. I was able to act like I had it before I got it.

Attitude determines altitude

I found it ironic that principles I had learned and taught over the years kept coming to my remembrance. I've taught this principle time and again because attitude is so important. Attitude determines altitude means that your attitude or outlook on life has a direct impact on your level of success and achievement. I had to remember that a positive attitude enabled me to overcome obstacles and reach greater altitudes. I also had to remember that having a positive attitude can also inspire and motivate others. A positive attitude could still make a big difference in my life and in the lives of those around me, if I would just change my attitude. How? I had to replace negative thoughts with positive ones.

In Proverbs 23:7, Solomon said, *For as he thinketh in his heart, so is he...* Therefore, if I think positive thoughts, I receive positive outcomes. If I think negative thoughts, I receive negative outcomes because my outcomes are directly affected by my thoughts. So, if I wanted things to change for the better, I was going to have to recalibrate my mind, which involved consciously re-ordering my thoughts and attitudes. It would not be easy, but I knew what had to be done. Aside from the wisdom I continued to receive through daily devotion and ministry studies, these steps, gleaned from self-help literature, also helped me advance to my next level:

1. *I began to identify negative thought patterns.* I had to develop a consciousness about my own negativity. I stopped beating myself up, stopped thinking in terms of "I can't." I began each day with prayer, then spent much of it complaining. Humility was the key, because this change took mental and spiritual effort – sometimes I laughed at myself and felt like a child, but I was determined. I "fined" myself if I heard myself doubting my capabilities. What I had to do was identify the thought patterns that were holding me back, and face them down.
2. *I had to challenge negative thoughts.* I was in my own way. Once I identified some of my negative thoughts, I questioned their validity. The phrase, "Too blessed to be stressed," comes to mind. I

asked myself if there was evidence to support these thoughts. Yes, there might be, but so what? That's when I started to seriously count my blessings: 3 grown, healthy, loving children topping the list.

3. *I replaced negative thoughts with positive ones.* I continued to reinforce positivity in my life by reexamining myself and the people, places, and things closest to me. I knew to surround myself with positive people in nurturing environments. I replaced those negative thoughts with prayers and "anytime" affirmations, and reflected on them often. My positive thoughts made me more conscious of humility and sincerity in relationships.

4. *I stopped practicing self-condemnation and turned that energy around.* I had been so down on myself. I reflected on the opportunities I had let slip through my fingers and vowed to close that door. I have been re-directed. It is OK for me to acknowledge and appreciate the positive aspects of my life, including my faith, my education, and my career. I love my family and I know that I am loved. This turnaround has helped reframe my mindset and cultivate a positive outlook.

5. *I started surrounding myself with positivity.* It's not just church where I find positive people. I examined my circle of people, places, and events. I wanted to ensure that I was being fed, spiritually and otherwise. This includes what I choose in media

content, entertainment, sports, or educational pursuits. Surround yourself with positive influences, whether it be supportive friends, Gospel music, motivational books, or inspirational content. "Satan is busy," we often say. This step helps keep him at bay.

6. *I began to practice self-care*. This last step was one of the most important because I neglected myself for so long. I was not taking consciously good care of myself. Aside from being involved with my kids and their busy lives, I love improving my physical and mental well-being by engaging in activities that bring me joy and relaxation: exercise, spa care, meditation, reading, and traveling. Minding myself keeps me healthier; taking care of myself improved my overall mindset.

Going to another altitude with your attitude requires work. Recalibration takes time and consistent effort, because it is a continuing process of rewiring your thought patterns and developing a more empowering mindset. I learned to be patient with myself. I also took time to celebrate my progress along the way.

I don't look like what I have been through.

*Now unto Him who is able to keep us...*Jude uttered these words in his letter to the church, people who had lost their way. When they received the gospel, they received it with open hearts and adhered to the principles they were taught. For some reason, the teaching did not stick. When they were presented with another form of teaching, they were lured away from that which they knew. So, the writer challenged them by asking, Who hindered you? What happened to cause them to be drawn away from what they learned? After this rebuke, the writer reminded them that there is still One who is able to keep them. Jude doesn't only speak about God's ability, he also implies his availability, and that He is able to keep them from falling.

There are times that we need divine aid to help us persist through the trials and temptations of life. I have learned that temptations are tailor-made. The enemy will not tempt us with anything that does not have the potential of causing us to fall. Thankfully, Jude lets us know that we have insurance in those situations. Because when times like those come, God is able to keep us. In the Greek, the word keep is "phulasso." It literally means to preserve. Something that would have spoiled gains a new lease on life because it has been preserved, it has been kept. Jude is saying that God can preserve us in times when we would have fallen.

The only reason I'm still here is that I have been kept. I have fallen many times. I remember God reassuring me one day by saying that my fall came before I got up, so I didn't have far to fall. Thankfully, none of my falls were fatal. And because they weren't fatal, they weren't final. Instead, *the falls became fuel and furthered me towards my future.* It's crazy to say and might seem oxymoronic, but my falls have proven to be fruitful. Why?

Because I don't look like what I have been through. You can go through the metaphorical fire of life and not smell like smoke. It's just as interesting when you can go through the flood yet show no remnants of water. That's what happens when you stop allowing your trials to make you *bitter* and start learning from them, allowing those trials to make you *better*. Put every experience in a faith file and run with the reality of knowing that if He did it then, He can and will do it again. We just have to trust Him. And I've learned how to trust Him.

In fact, I've graduated from saying that I don't look like what I have been through to saying that I look exactly like everything I've gone through. That's why I tell people when I go through the vicissitudes of life. I want them to know because I want them to see when I made the transition from victim to victor once God has given me victory. The same vicissitudes that were once vices and voices, God has now given me victory over. And that's why I put it out in the atmosphere, so that when it happens, everyone will know that it had to be God. There is no way I could have done it by myself.

I learned not to lean to my own understanding, but to acknowledge Him in all my ways. That's why He directs my path. That's why the Scripture that asserts the steps of a good man are ordered by the Lord has proven to be true in my life (Prov. 16:9). I am exactly where He wants me to be. So, whether or not I look like what I've been through, I went through it. Sometimes I went kicking and screaming, but I went. Sometimes I went knucking and bucking, but I went. Sometimes I cried and sometimes I laughed, but I went through it. Guess what! Every round goes higher, and I am ready to go higher.

I must change the countenance of the man in purple...

In 2004, a few courageous people and I established Bridging the Gap Ministries in Dalton, GA. Never in a million years would I have thought I would be a church planter. I once envisioned myself going into an established church, preaching, teaching, casting vision, and growing that church. That was how I saw my future evolving. Wrong! Evidently, God had other plans. Nothing was wrong with what I saw because I had good intentions. The outcomes I sought were outstanding and would positively affect the world. But my plans weren't God's plans. That has been one of the biggest issues with the things God shows me. I always see the beginning and the end, but don't always see the process. I have always seen myself being successful, but never fully understood how that success would be attained. Because I was called to ministry, I assumed that success would come through ministry. So, if I was going to be a planter, I was going to plant big. I wanted to plant churches in several cities. I learned that principle watching my father in ministry, Bishop Kenneth L Robinson.

I believe it was early 2008, and we had moved to Conyers, a little town east of Atlanta. Hard times caused me to move my family there. Nikki and I enrolled the children in school and signed them up for activities. I embraced the culture of that community and made some positive connections. Conyers seemed like the perfect place to start my next ministry. Rewind. I tried to start a second ministry in Marietta that didn't work out. Anyway, we started worshipping in a hotel on Sunday nights. I would lead a worship service in Dalton on Sunday mornings and in Conyers on Sunday evenings. We had powerful worship. Gifted musicians and singers would come in and help. Men and women of God also came to join and support us. The parachurch community came alive in worship; they wanted more God. They didn't care where they worshipped; they just wanted to worship.

One woman stands out in my memory. One evening after church, she came toward me as if she wanted to have a conversation. This was not uncommon; I was used to people doing that. Some wanted to talk; some wanted to encourage me. Some knew our struggle, so they would sow seeds into our lives in the form of money. Well, when she came forward, she had what looked like money, folded up in her hand. Well, it wasn't real money. Instead, it was a $1 million-dollar bill, along with a prophecy. In the prophecy, she described a vision in which a man dressed in purple was staring at me. He represented some type of royalty and had with him copious riches. She said he wanted to give them to me but for some reason, could not. She said she could see a look of concern on his face.

I heard her words back then, but somewhere along the way, I lost sight of what she said. In fact, this prophecy was lodged deep in the recesses of my mind until the other day, when I was trying to think of a way to conclude this book. Unpacking a dusty box, I ran across a leather wallet I had not seen in years. In the wallet was the fake $1 million bill the woman had given me 15 years earlier. It was only then that I remembered that powerful moment I had just casually passed over. Thankfully, God's promises do not come with expiration dates. If He said it, that settles it; our job is seize each promise. If the man in purple was looking at me then, he is looking at me now, and his riches have gained interest. If they were meant for me, they are mine. They are my destiny, custom-made, just for me. My role is to change the countenance of the man in purple, to make him smile. That is why I am on the path to better.

www.ingramcontent.com/pod-product-compliance
Lightning Source LLC
Chambersburg PA
CBHW051531120626
46551CB00012B/1167